LOVING FROM A DISTANCE

How to Make Your Romantic Long Distance Relationship Work

Nora Williams

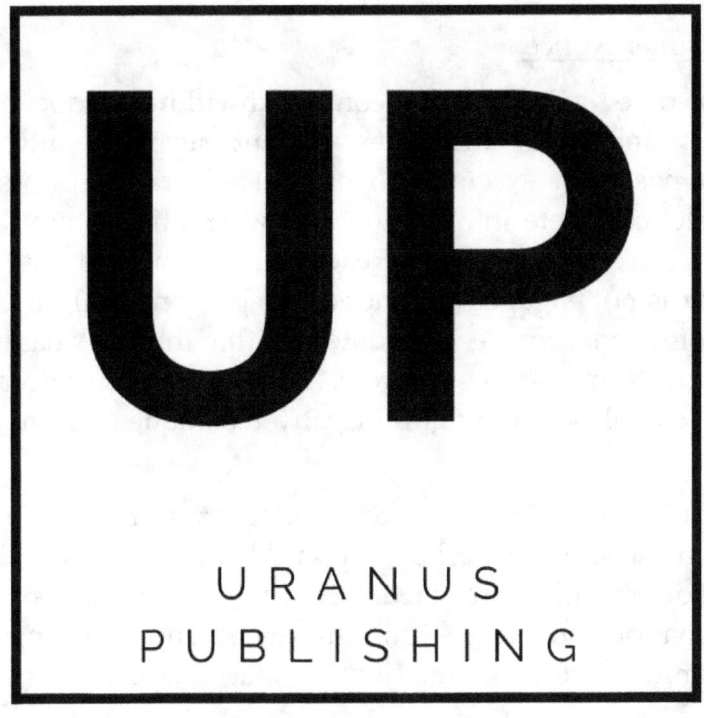

All rights reserved © 2021 by Nora Williams

...

ISBN: 978-1-915218-02-5

First Edition: October 2021

This book is copyright protected. It is only for personal use. You cannot amend, distribute, sell, use, quote, or paraphrase any part of this book's content without the author or publisher's consent. All pictures contained in this book come from the author's personal archive or copyright-free stock websites (Pixabay, Pexel, Freepix, Unsplash, StockSnap, etc.).

Disclaimer Notice:

Please note the information contained within this document is for educational and entertainment purposes only. All effort has been executed to present accurate, up-to-date, reliable, complete information. No warranties of any kind are declared or implied. Readers acknowledge that the author is not engaged in rendering legal, financial, medical or professional advice. The content within this book has been derived from various sources. Please consult a licensed professional before attempting any techniques outlined in this book.

By reading this document, the reader agrees that under no circumstances is the author responsible for any losses, direct or indirect, that are incurred due to the use of the information contained within this document, including, but not limited to, errors, omissions, or inaccuracies.

The trademarks used are without any consent, and the publication of the trademark is without permission or backing by the trademark owner. All trademarks and brands within this book are for clarifying purposes only and are owned by the owners themselves, not affiliated with this document.

HUDSON BAY
ALBERTA
MANITOBA
CANADA
STATES
GULF OF MEXICO
CENTRAL AMERICA
Vancouver
Seattle
Olympia
Helena
Butte
Pendleton
Salem
Eugene
Boise
Sacramento
LOS ANGELES
Phoenix
Tucson
Santa Fé
Oklahoma City
Amarillo
Dallas
Topeka
Kansas City
Wichita
Omaha
Lincoln
Des Moines
Springfield
Cincinnati
Louisville
Memphis
Atlanta
Charleston
Jacksonville
St Augustine
New Orleans
Galveston
Brownsville
Norfolk
Wilmington
Raleigh
Richmond
WASHINGTON
Baltimore
Boston
Portland
OTTAWA
Duluth
Aberdeen
Deadwood
Jackson
Pensacola
Key West
Eagle Pass
Laredo
San Quintin
JAMAICA
MEXICO

TABLE OF CONTENTS

INTRODUCTION 1

LONG DISTANCE RELATIONSHIPS 5

Characteristics 5

LDRs with family and friends 6

Keeping Family Relationships Alive 7

The impact of geographic separation on the well-being of children 8

Long-distance military relations 10

Statistics in the United States 10

Methods of communication 11

Maintenance practices in relationships 12

COMMON ISSUES IN LONG-DISTANCE RELATIONSHIPS 15

Inadequate communication 16

Jealousy 17

Loneliness 18

Moving away 18

Time 19

Trust issues 20

REAL STATISTICS ABOUT LONG-DISTANCE RELATIONSHIPS 23

Some interesting numbers 24

How long will my long-distance relationship last? 27

HOW TO HANDLE YOUR FIRST TIME IN A LONG DISTANCE RELATIONSHIP 39

Agree On Expectations 40

Maintain Consistency, Especially When It Comes to Communication 41

Keep a safe distance. 42

To each other, be kind and truthful. 43

Don't shy away from conflict. 43

When you're not with your partner, learn more about yourself. 44

It's possible that not every trip will be fantastic. 44

Create an LDR budget. 45

Keep in mind that your partner has a life you may or may not be a part of. 46

Maintain a realistic perspective rather than a romantic one. .. 46

Be adaptable. 47

Make sure you've got a game plan in place. 48

TRIED AND TRUE TIPS FOR YOUR LDR 49

Tip 1: Expect to put in twice as much effort as you did previously. 50

Tip 2: Make some ground rules for when you and your partner will see each other. 50

Tip 3: Keep in touch with each other throughout the day by calling and texting. 51

Tip 4: Remember to set up regular Skype dates. 51

Tip #5: Take a step back and consider the broad picture. 52

Tip #6: Make a big deal out of everything. 52

Tip #7: Get an airline-miles-earning credit card. 53

Tip 8: Don't be concerned if your visits aren't perfect. 53

"I DON'T KNOW WHAT WE CAN TALK ABOUT ANYMORE" 55

Fun Questions to Ask Your Partner When You are in an LDR 55

Dos and Don'ts When It Comes to Falling in Love and Long-Distance Dating 62

HOW TO MAKE YOUR LONG DISTANCE RELATIONSHIP WORK 69

Examine your communication requirements. 71

Keep your independence. 71

When at all feasible, stick to your 'meeting' times. 72

Change up your communication methods. 72

Make the most of your communication. 73

Don't overlook closeness. 74

Exchange physical mementos of one another. 75

When possible, spend time together. 75

Even if you can't physically be there, "be there." 76

Form a strong bond by supporting each other's goals. 78

Find a way to stay in touch when you're away. 79

Learn how to deal with pressing situations both online and in person. 79

Concentrate on the advantages of long-distance travel. 80

Respect each other's reasons for being apart. 81

Make a long-term plan for integrating your worlds when the time is appropriate. 82

To keep your expectations in check, establish some ground rules. 83

Make filthy jokes at each other. 84

Collaborate on projects. 85

Carry out identical actions. 85

Maintain an open line of communication with one another. 87

You should be aware of each other's schedules. 88

Give the other individual a sentimental item to hold on to. 88

Make sure you have a good messaging app. 89

Maintain an optimistic attitude. 89

LONG-DISTANCE ACTIVITIES FOR COUPLES 91

What to stay away from 95

Keeping your emotions and feelings to yourself 97

IDENTIFYING AND RESOLVING COMMON PROBLEMS 99

- *Relationship expectations vary.* 99
- *Issues of trust* 100
- *Conflict avoidance* 101
- *Feeling disconnected from each other's life* 102
- *Expectations regarding money* 103

THE MATTER OF CHOICE IN LONG DISTANCE RELATIONSHIPS 105

LONG DISTANCE RELATIONSHIPS - FAQS 111

POSITIVE HABITS TO IMPROVE YOUR LDR 131

- *Keep a positive attitude!* 131
- *Re-Learn What It Means to Be Intimate* 132
- *There are some things that must be said.* 135
- *Refrain from isolating yourself!* 136
- *Be Prepared for Disappointment.* 136
- *Lastly, master the art of long-distance sex.* 137

CONCLUSION 139

INTRODUCTION

"Absence is to love what wind is to fire; it extinguishes the small, it inflames the great." – Roger de Bussy-Rabutin

Is it possible to have romance in a long-distance relationship? Of course, people have been enjoying long-distance love relationships since the dawn of romance. However, when someone has to be away for an extended amount of time, the romance must be long-distance for the relationship to continue. Find out how to maintain a loving long-distance relationship.

You must first understand what romance is to know how to have romance in a long-distance relationship. Giving someone flowers and a card might be romantic. A candle-lit supper with champagne and soft love music in the background could make your lover feel good on the inside. I may also be referring to a romantic evening with your sweetheart. Romance can be as simple as telling someone you love them.

As we've seen, romance may mean many various ways. It all boils down to making that special someone feel loved and unique when it comes down to it. A candle-lit romantic supper isn't the same as the one you'd have with just anyone. It's the only one you'd make for your special someone. The fundamentals of romance are nearly identical in a passionate long-distance relationship.

The only distinction between a conventional romance and a romantic long-distance relationship is the distance. There is a considerable distance between you two, and you are no longer physically connected. So you'll have to develop fresh ways to express your love and show your partner how important they are to you.

In a romantic long-distance relationship, there are many ways to express your love. The most significant is verbal. Talking on the phone is a good way to connect. You can even see this person using the internet. You can speak, see, and write to your partner using new technologies that can be used over the internet. You can also send your partner romantic virtual cards and gifts to enhance your romantic experience. The most amazing part about these technologies is that they are entirely free to use so far you have access to the internet and the necessary hardware.

Communication is essential in any relationship, but especially in a romantic long-distance relationship.

That is all you have due to the distance. As a result, it's critical to communicate with your partner regularly. Because these services are free, using these new internet technologies will help a lot today. You can utilize voice and see real-time videos of your partner. This is the most effective technique to stay in touch when you're apart.

LONG DISTANCE RELATIONSHIPS

A long-distance relationship (LDR) or long-distance romantic relationship (LDRR) is a romantic partnership between two people who live far apart geographically. Separation geographically and a lack of face-to-face contact are challenges for LDR partners. LDRs are most common among college students, accounting for between 25% and 50% of all partnerships. Even though that many LDRs have been documented in student populations, long-distance relationships remain an understudied phenomenon.

Characteristics

LDRs differ qualitatively from geographically close relationships, which are those in which the parties may see each other daily. Long-distance romantic relationships face the following unique challenges, according to Rohlfing (1995):

- Difficulty keeping geographically close friendships when in long-distance romantic relationships

- Difficulty evaluating the state of a relationship from a distance

LDRs with family and friends

Long-distance relationships aren't always romantic. Individuals' ties with family and friends become long-distance when they go away to school. According to Pew Internet (2004), 79 percent of adult respondents in the United States use the Internet to communicate with family and friends. According to Pew Internet, college students will have stronger social relationships with their peers than with their family members due to new technology. Examining email among college students aids in investigating how the Internet affects college students emotionally and socially.

Migration has increasingly become a characteristic of contemporary society due to the significant effect of globalization and advancements in transportation and communication technologies. As a result, transnational families, in which family members live in different regions, and countries yet share a sense of collective connection beyond national lines, are becoming more frequent. Thus, for example, children may choose to leave home to study abroad, parents may opt to leave home in search of better opportunities and income, and siblings may opt to pursue separate life paths around the world.

Keeping Family Relationships Alive

Researchers discovered that geographically separated family members exchanged all types of care and support that proximate families did. That includes financial, practical, personal, housing, and emotional or moral support, resulting from a qualitative study of 50 interviews with adult migrant children in Australia and their parents in Italy, Ireland, and the Netherlands. As indicated by Loretta Baldassar, the main factor in supporting and keeping up transnational family connections was the trading of passion, including moral help among parents and kids. In addition, the growing usage of Internet technology has facilitated emotional exchange between distant family members and provided them with everyday access to low-cost long-distance communication to keep in touch.

Cao (2013) conducted a series of interviews with fourteen people who were frequently in contact with family members in different time zones, including the United Kingdom, the United States, Canada, and China. According to the study, remote family members relied largely on synchronous techniques for virtual contact, including telephone and Internet audio/video calls (e.g., Skype) instead of asynchronous ones like email or text messaging. Cao considers real-time involvement from synchronous communication to be a vital component of emotional support because it creates a sense of presence, connectivity, and dedication among family members. However, it is important to emphasize that Internet technologies have not replaced the usage of older, less useful forms of communication, such as letters, cards, gifts, and photographs, which transnational families still use to express their concern and affection.

According to research, people maintain intimate ties with different family members by adopting diverse communication styles. People frequently contact immediate family members such as parents and children, but less frequently and regularly with other family members such as siblings across time zones. Siblings are said to feel less forced to contact one other regularly, especially among the younger generation, and instead prefer ad hoc communication, such as updating each other's status via instant chats.

The impact of geographic separation on the well-being of children

A large percentage of parents go to another country to pursue a job, leaving their children behind in their nation. These parents aim to give better opportunities for their children in the future. However, the effects of parents' labor migration on the growth of their children left behind are mixed, depending on various conditions. The effects of transnational living arrangements on children's well-being vary. For example, researchers found that left-behind children may profit financially from the remittances their parents send home while suffering emotionally from long-term separation after interviewing 755 Mexican households with at least one family member who had moved to the US.

Lahaie, Hayes, Piper, and Heymann (2009) found similar results in a correlational study utilizing a representative sample of transnational families in Mexico and the United States to investigate the association between parental migration and children's mental health outcomes. Furthermore, whether the mother or father migrates for employment has an impact. Considering traditional family gender roles, children tended to face greater emotional problems from transnational motherhood than paternity, based on interviews and observations with Filipina transnational households. In addition, the effects of parent migration on children's psychological well-being vary across the country.

Graham and Jordan (2011) showed that children of migrant fathers in Indonesia and Thailand were more likely than children from non-migrant families to suffer from poor psychological health, while the findings did not replicate in children from PNG. Children's growth is significantly influenced by special care arrangements for left-behind children, such as asking extended family members for assistance in caring for them. When placed side by side with other children with care arrangements, Lahaie et al. (2009) discovered that kids who took care of themselves had a higher likelihood of exhibiting behavioral and educational issues. The sensation of being abandoned by parents is one reason why youngsters engage in risky activities such as dropping out of school or joining a gang as a form of vengeance.

Long-distance military relations

Before and during the deployment, the partners of military troops stationed abroad are under great stress. The distinction between a military LDR and a typical LDR is that. In contrast, a regular LDR has more communication, a military LDR's communication is either unexpected and restricted by military regulations, or there isn't much time to communicate.

Because of the communication limits and the general deployment process, the spouse at home feels lonely and worried about maintaining the strong relationship moving ahead. The fact that the military member is being deployed to a conflict zone where their life is at risk adds to the emotional turmoil. The partner will experience various emotional issues throughout the deployment, including anxiety, loss, denial, rage, despair, and acceptance.

Statistics in the United States

According to a 2005 survey, 14 to 15 million people in the United States were thought to be long-distance relationships. In 2015, nearly 14 million people were identified as being in a long-distance relationship. Long-distance relationships account for 32.5 percent of college relationships. In a long-distance relationship, the average distance traveled is 125 miles. Long-distance couples call each other every 2.7 days on average. Couples in long-distance relationships visit each other 1.5 times per month on average. Couples in long-distance relationships can also expect to live together after 14 months of dating.

Approximately 40% of long-distance couples split up, with the most common onset of issues occurring around 4.5 months into the relationship. Also, 70 percent of couples in a long-distance relationship break up due to unplanned circumstances and events. About 75 percent of couples in long-distance relationships end up being engaged at some point in the relationship. After marriage, approximately 10% of couples maintain a long-distance relationship. In the United States alone, almost 3.75 million married couples are involved in long-distance relationships.

Methods of communication

New communication technology, such as cellular phone plans, make long-distance communication easier than ever before. Long-distance relationships were not as common before the popularity of internet dating. The primary means of communication between the romance lovers was usually telephone conversations or correspondence via mail. When asked how often they used the Internet on a normal day, American citizens reported 56 percent sending or reading email, 10% sending instant messaging, and 9% utilizing an online social network such as Facebook or Twitter, according to Pew Internet. On the other hand, long-distance relationships have expanded in popularity since the birth of the Internet, as they have become easier to maintain thanks to contemporary technology. Finally, talking and creating realistic goals can aid in the prevention of detachment and loss of touch.

As the number of long-distance relationships grows, so do various techniques to help intimate couples live apart. Some technologies have attempted to imitate co-located activities such as hugging and kissing from a distance. These technologies have had minimal success thus far.

Long-distance relationships can be maintained by couples that engage in routine, deliberate relational maintenance practices and utilize social media. The routine and strategic maintenance techniques are positive interactions, openness (discussing relationships and one's feelings directly), confidence (confirming the partner about the relationship and the future), network (relying on support and other people's love), shared tasks (performing common tasks), and conflict management.

Maintenance practices in relationships

Intimate connection partners are always striving to improve their bond. They can make their partner happy in a variety of ways, which will strengthen their overall relationship. Individual behaviors have a significant impact on relationship satisfaction and long-term viability. Researchers discovered systems of intimate partner maintenance practices. Maintenance behaviors can be divided into seven categories: affirmations about their partner's love and commitment, openness in discussing their feelings, conflict management, good interactions, task sharing, giving advice to their partner, and using social media for support (Dainton, 2000; Stafford, Dainton, & Haas, 2000).

Partners utilize three types of sustaining behaviors to deal with separation, according to Dindia and Emmers-Sommer (2006). "Prospective actions, such as saying goodbye to the partner, address expected separation; introspective behaviors, which are communication when the partners are separated; and retrospective behaviors, which are essentially face-to-face communication, which reaffirms connection after separation."

In 2006, Indira and Emmers-Sommer published Indira and Emmers-Sommer (Dindia and Emmers-Sommer). The relationship continuity constructional units are what they're called (RCCUs). The RCCUs and maintenance behaviors are linked to increased relationship satisfaction and commitment (Pistole et al., 2010).

COMMON ISSUES IN LONG-DISTANCE RELATIONSHIPS

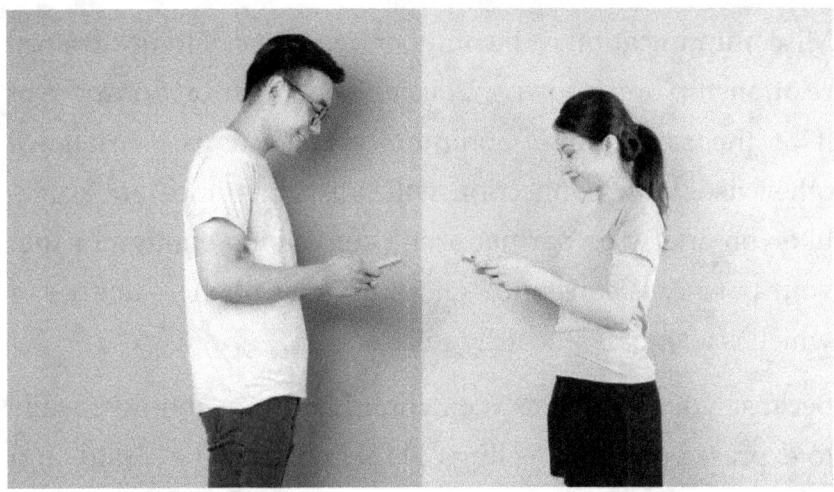

Everyone will have the opportunity to experience a long-distance relationship at some point in their lives, but if you are one of the few who will not consider yourself fortunate! It is definitely difficult to be in a relationship, let alone a long-distance one where you and your partner are separated by a thousand miles, but it will not be difficult if you are with the right person.

Every relationship has ups and downs; it is not all rainbows and butterflies, and it is especially tough to mend relationship problems when you and your boyfriend or girlfriend are separated, but don't worry! As you read on, you will see that these "downs" in your relationships are fairly typical and that there are answers.

Here are six frequent long-distance relationship issues and their solutions.

Inadequate communication

Miscommunication is the number one cause of long-distance relationship breakdowns. You can't have less of it or more of it at the same time. Communication must be balanced; otherwise, your connection will fail. Sometimes you'll feel like you and your partner aren't conversing enough or that your partner is constantly checking their phone – neither of which is a sign of a healthy relationship.

Because your partner is your confidante, you should be able to express your true feelings to them. Do not be afraid, and do not suppress your emotions, since if they truly love you, they will understand. If you are not comfortable with your partner hanging out with a certain person, do not be afraid to express your concerns to them. If your partner is now willing to share their concerns with you because they do not want to bother you, show them that you are eager to assist.

Balance is essential, which is why you and your partner should effectively communicate with each other to avoid miscommunication. You don't have to talk to each other every minute of every day because the most important thing is that when you chat, you're both able to relay your feelings and concerns and talk about them openly rather than keeping them to yourselves. Remember that it is better to have said it than not to have said it and later regret it.

Jealousy

Every relationship contains the green-eyed monster. It lives in the heart and perceives the world through the eyes of the person. It is very normal to experience the green-eyed monster, commonly known as jealousy, within you. Jealousy is also a very typical issue in any relationship, long-distance or otherwise.

The green-eyed monster has no mercy, whether it's the pretty secretary your guy works with or the nerdy classmate your girlfriend is working on a project with. It is illogical, clingy, and, most importantly, it can take over your entire body. If you continue to feed your jealousy, it will likely take over your brain and cause you to do stupid things like contacting your spouse every hour or banning them from going out with anyone at all.

Never, ever succumb to the green-eyed monster. If you have no reason to be jealous, then don't be jealous! It would help if you had enough faith in your relationship to avoid making up problems in your head. If you scrutinize every detail, such as "Why did she text him if he has the reports?" or "Why is he working on that project with her?" you will never be able to relax. People who don't have motives should not be given them. The most important thing to do to keep the green-eyed monster at bay is to not feed it.

Loneliness

Loneliness is a cherished old friend who visits every now and then, but loneliness is not always welcome in long-distance relationships. There will be occasions when you feel lonely, but this is a pretty common feeling. Loneliness exists because your companion is not present. Looking on the bright side, you may be lonely because you crave the affection you feel when your lover is present.

A variety of factors can cause loneliness. For example, you and your lover may live in separate time zones, so when they are sleeping, you're wide awake and eating breakfast. It could also be due to hectic work schedules since, even if you're in a relationship, you're still two different individuals, or it could be one of the most fundamental reasons – you simply miss your spouse.

Loneliness can be alleviated by placing everyday reminders of your mate about your home. For example, you can display picture frames from memorable occasions, the quilt blanket they gave you last Christmas, or reread the love messages your partner sent you! Remember that even if your partner is not physically present, you may sense their love through the mementos and presents you share.

Moving away

Some relationships have ended because the two people who were once in love "drifted apart." The process of drifting apart is analogous to a snowball sliding downhill. It begins little, then grows into a massive snowball poised to destroy any relationship in its path.

It can start with something as simple as returning your messages late or not returning your messages at all, progressing to canceled date plans or video chats, not picking up calls. Then your partner will suddenly contact you and tell you one of the most overused cliches in romance history: "It's not you, it's me" or "I think the distance between us caused us to drift apart."

To avoid drifting apart, ensure that the foundation of your relationship is strong, which means that it was not based on falsehoods and mistrust, but most importantly, ensure that you know yourself. Most people who leave a relationship do so because they have finally learned who they are, and you are not always a part of their plans. So, before you enter into any relationship, make sure that both you and your partner are secure in their own identities. Never look for someone who makes you feel whole because you should be whole before that person comes along.

Time

Time can be an unfair adversary because it is something you cannot fight against. Unfortunately, people in long-distance relationships sometimes become so preoccupied with their own life that they neglect to spend time with their partners. Others are so preoccupied with their employment that they neglect to make time in their hectic schedules for their loved ones. Unfortunately, this does not only happen to couples but also to families and friends.

Time is an even more formidable foe when your lover lives on another continent and is separated by time zones. It can be difficult to maintain communication, especially if you are at work all day and when you call your partner, they are already asleep. A lack of communication can breed mistrust and even jealousy. Nobody wants to arouse the green-eyed monster.

Scheduling time is one of the most effective methods to combat it. This may appear monotonous because it becomes a routine, but it works! Look for the best time for you and your partner to spend time together. If your boyfriend or girlfriend is only a few miles away, make time to visit him or her every other weekend, because there is no such thing as "no time" for the people you care about.

Trust issues

It's understandable if the distance makes you nervous about your relationship. There are times when people are just beginning out in their relationships and are swept into the whirlwind that is life, and they end up at opposite ends of the spectrum. They did not spend enough time together to get to know each other and build a solid foundation of trust. Sometimes a person falls in love with someone they met online. Mistrust can be caused by a lack of relationships and an increase in people between two people.

The only way out of this is to take a leap of faith. Love is a game of chance, and you must roll the dice. There is no sure way to tell if you can truly trust someone. Do not constantly bug your partner. Please give them the personal space they require because the last thing you want to do is make them feel like a confined animal. The only thing you need to tell yourself is that you believe in the love you share with your spouse and that this reasons enough for you to trust them.

Love is difficult. It takes a lot of dedication and hard effort to make it rewarding. It's not always all smiles and dates. There will be times when you and your partner will fight and perhaps despise one other over trivial matters. However, you should never give up on the individuals you care about. Even when your lover is the most difficult to love, you choose to love him or her regardless of the circumstances. The essential thing to remember is that this happens in every relationship and that there is always an answer to all problems!

REAL STATISTICS ABOUT LONG-DISTANCE RELATIONSHIPS

College is commencing, which means that many students' relationships are going to change. Many people will have their first long-distance relationships in the coming months as they and their significant others transfer to other universities. Will they, however, be able to stay together in the long run?

The cycle from high school relationship to long-distance college relationship to breakup is so regular that there's even slang for it: "the turkey drop." That's what it's called when college students come home for Thanksgiving and split up with their high school lovers.

But not all high school romances conclude with a "turkey drop," or even terminate at all. In reality, more and more young couples are deciding to do long-distance work for a few years, or perhaps forever. Channa Bromley, Lead Coach at Relationship Hero, recently told Refinery29, "It's becoming a lot more widespread because the world is gradually becoming so much more accessible than what it used to be." "You have people going to various institutions and staying together, and when we receive promotions and career possibilities, they might not be in the same place as our partner."

Will your long-distance romance result in a breakup?

We can't answer that because it actually depends on each particular pair. But we can provide nine true data on long-distance relationships.

Some interesting numbers

Almost half of all daters are interested in long-distance relationships.

According to OkCupid research from 2019, 46% of women and 45% of men are open to a long-distance relationship with the right person.

Over half of all long-distance relationships last for more than a year.

According to a study conducted in 2018, 58 percent of Americans who have been in long-term relationships will stay together.

The largest issue is a lack of physical intimacy.

According to the same KIIROO survey, the absence of physical intimacy was the most challenging aspect of being in a long-distance relationship for 66% of respondents. In comparison, the lack of sex was the most difficult aspect for 31%.

A long-distance relationship will be the norm for most college students.

According to 2005 research, up to 75% of college students had been in a long-distance relationship at a point in their lives, and 35% of college students are currently in long-distance relationships.

Long-distance relationships, on average, do not endure as long.

According to a 2010 German study, the average longevity of a long-distance relationship is 2.9 years, which is not up to half of the 7.3 years of a proximal relationship.

Long-distance partnerships may be more stable.

Persons in long-distance relationships reported higher levels of idealism, happy memories, perceived agreement, communication quality, and even romantic love than people in geographically nearby relationships, according to a 2007 study.

...until they meet again.

According to the same survey, around one-third of long-distance couples split up within three months after reuniting.

Having a deadline increases satisfaction.

Students who didn't know whether they could ever live in a similar city as their accomplice detailed inclination "essentially more bothered, less fulfilled, and evaluated correspondence adapting methodologies as less supportive than the individuals who felt more sure about the get-together," as indicated by a 2007 investigation of undergrads in significant distance connections.

Relationship quality isn't determined by distance.

A 1995 study revealed "no significant differences" in relationship quality between 194 people in long-distance relationships and 190 people in proximal relationships, as evaluated by "self-reported levels of relationship satisfaction, intimacy, dyadic trust, and the degree of relationship advancement." Long-distance relationships have their own set of difficulties, yet they can be just as strong as proximal relationships.

Your romance does not have to stop just because you and your partner are going to different schools and potentially separate states.

Long-Distance Relationships: How Long Do They Last?

Long-distance relationships are difficult to maintain. You meet a person, fall in love, and decide to give a relationship a chance in the hopes of one day forging a future together. But then new job prospects or family duties present themselves, and you're suddenly faced with the prospect of spending the next few months — or even years — apart.

It's comforting to know that long-distance relationships aren't always doomed. Dr. Joshua Klapow, a clinical psychologist, told Elite Daily that long-distance relationships are difficult but not impossible. "Successful long-distance relationships happen every day, despite the hurdles," he stated. "Long-distance relationships are realistic if there is a strong emotional link, effort, and dedication to helping each partner feel safe, connected, and autonomous."

Significant distance relationship mentalities are by all accounts moving also. As per Refinery29, 46% of ladies and 45 percent of men are currently open to the possibility of a significant distance relationship if it's with the "ideal individual," as per information from dating site OkCupid, and another study uncovered that 58% of Americans in long haul connections would doubtlessly remain together.

How long will my long-distance relationship last?

While the average period of a relationship is 7.3 years, a German study found that long-distance relationships survive only around half or slightly under three years. Furthermore, while long-distance relationships may be more stable due to variables such as greater communication and happy memories, according to a published study in the Journal of Social and Personal Relationships in 2007, a third of couples split up within three months of reuniting and settling down together (via Refinery29).

Long-distance relationships can be difficult, but contemporary technology may help strengthen — or dissolve — links within a couple. EurekAlert! published the findings of a study on social media in the context of a long-distance relationship. "Those in long-distance relationships are bound to utilize a person to person communication locales," said the manager in boss Brenda K. Wiederhold, adding, "As significant distance connections become more normal and keep on succeeding, it turns out to be progressively important to comprehend the job that innovation plays in fortifying or harming a close connection."

So, how long does a long-distance relationship have a chance to last? A long-distance romance can become a lifetime connection with the correct tools and mindset – provided you and your partner work together to cultivate it.

There are ten signals that your long-distance romance is going to last.

Long-distance relationships can be healthy because of the seemingly limitless ways to communicate with loved ones (messaging, calling, Snapchatting, tweeting, tagging).

Maintaining a strong link with a spouse requires consistent communication, whether they are in another city, state, or country. When embarking on a long-distance relationship, though, there are other factors to consider.

Here are ten indicators that you and your spouse might be able to go the distance.

They want to know about your day.

Long-distance relationships are no exception. Texting is the easiest and convenient way to communicate with friends and family. It's a good idea to call or video chat once a week, but most of your communication will likely be done via text, especially if you and your partner have different schedules.

Obviously, it is critical to keep each other informed about advancements, accomplishments, and major events, but the importance of daily details should not be overlooked. Specifics help you comprehend your partner's emotions and fill in the blanks in their life that you may otherwise overlook.

Ask questions and inject some personality into your posts. You'll feel closer to each other, and the adjustment from daily messaging to face-to-face talk will be more seamless once you're reunited.

They use the postal service to send packages.

Even though an Instagram message is sent in a flash, there is something inexplicably romantic about receiving letters from a partner. A phone notification will never compare to the joy of opening a piece of mail from someone you care about, whether it's a parcel or a handwritten letter.

Flowers, chocolates, and cards are timeless, but a personal touch now and again demonstrates that your partner is aware of your preferences. You realize your partner is in it for the long stretch if they gift you dinosaur-molded espresso cups, a case of your #1 tea, or a customized mixtape. Remember to say thanks to them with your stand-out presents that help you to remember them.

They tell their friends and relatives about you.

Meeting your partner's family is crucial in any relationship, but some long-distance couples cannot achieve this until they live together. Whether or not you get the opportunity to meet their family, your significant other telling their family about you is a good signal of the future of your relationship.

Similarly, if they tell you about their family and give you updates on their parents, siblings, and grandparents, it suggests they're bridging the gap between you and their loved ones. If they don't have a biological family, they could develop a sense of belonging among their pals. The critical component is introducing you to people they respect, whether in conversation or in person. This is a strong indication that they are proud of their relationship with you and want to tell it to their friends and family.

They listen.

Without the luxury of physical touch and intimacy, the bulk of a long-distance relationship boils down to various forms of talking and listening. Listening is more than stillness on the other end of the line as you ramble about your day. Listening is an exercise that must be done every day.

If you comment that your back has been sore, an attentive person will review your misery and get some information about your back following an especially exhausting day. In addition, an attentive person will attempt to recollect the associates that make you insane and the boisterous canine that keeps you conscious around evening time.

Listening isn't such an extensive amount of memory game as it is a purposeful exertion associated with your life. For example, they don't need to recollect your manager's name, yet in the event that they review that your boss caused you to stay late on your birthday, that exhibits that they've been tuning in.

You're able to work through arguments together.

Long-distance relationships are prone to misunderstandings, conflict, and natural division, just like any other partnership. However, when individuals remain near their partner for most of their day, disputes are broken down out of a simple need to continue cohabitating.

The key to dealing with disputes from a distance is communicating how you feel. Magazines and blogs may provide "tricks" or "tips" to fixing relationship problems, but the easiest approach is nearly always speaking openly and simply about what you need from your spouse.

Vanessa Hudgens, who is presently dating actor Austin Butler over long-distance, advised People magazine that the secret to solving conflicts is simply communicating openly with your spouse. Hudgens stated, "Always bring it up and just talk about it. Uncensor yourself and just be open."

If they say anything that makes you angry, express your hurt and know why they said it. It could be a misunderstanding, or they could have a different viewpoint than you, but the essential thing is that they are aware of your distress and have the opportunity to apologize.

They have faith in you.

Jealousy is a natural human emotion, yet it frequently manifests itself in unreasonable behavior. In a relationship, the distinction between experiencing it and expressing it is critical. There'd be many nights and weekends where the two of you will find themselves in a sea of liquor and strangers at bars, clubs, and parties.

Seeing a photo of your lover with inebriated strangers or new friends can make you feel insecure. Consider your envy, let it wash over you, and then let it go. At the end of the day, if you and your partner trust each other, you have nothing to fear.

The authors of "The Long-Distance Relationship Survival Guide," Chris Bell and Katie-Brauer Bell, who have dated long-distance themselves, stress the necessity of being faithful and trusting that your partner would do the same. They emphasize how "fidelity is a natural extension of trust and honesty" and that "all three are equally crucial to the success of a long-distance relationship."

Presuming that your partner is cheating on you without cause is, in the end, an insult to their love for you. You will be able to overcome innumerable challenges in the future if they treat you with the same respect and confidence.

They make room for you.

When you're dating someone who lives hundreds, if not thousands, of miles away, it might feel like you're living two lives at once, which isn't always a terrible thing. Every relationship necessitates the development of independence and personality. In some ways, you have the edge over other couples because you have mastered the concept of leaving enough distance between you and your partner.

People can feel confined by their relationships if they don't have their own activities, interests, or buddy groups. Self-care is essential, as is finding activities that make you happy outside of your spouse.

Shannon Smith, a relationship specialist with the online dating website Plenty of Fish, told Business Insider, "Self-care and personal growth can make you a better person and partner – a huge component to helping a long-distance relationship (and any relationship) work."

"Take a class, prioritize your health, arrange a time with friends, or pick up a fantastic book you've meant to read," she continued.

Alternatively, it is critical to share with your partner so that they can rejoice with you and assist you in weathering your storms. Finding a balance between your identity as a person and your identity as a partner will lead to long-term happiness for both of you.

Every visit serves as a reminder of why the trip is worthwhile.

The average pair visits each other 1.5 times a month, according to Dr. Guldner of The Center for Study of LDRs. Partners may have to go months without seeing each other in some circumstances. And, for long-distance relationships that start on the internet, it can take years for couples to meet in person.

Though living apart can be lonely at times, one of the advantages of long-distance dating is the special kind of delight that both partners experience when they see each other. They are able to discuss their favorite local sites and activities that enrich their everyday lives after a long time apart.

It's also a terrific reason to go on trips and vacations with your friends, whether you meet midway or travel to a new location.

Even if they are few and far between, these weekends and visits serve as a reminder of why you chose to date long-distance in the first place.

They discuss the future in precise terms.

It's natural for couples to fantasize about how their lives will be when the distance between them ends. Still, it's critical to talk about specifics with your partner to become solid and stable your future together.

Of course, no person can possibly predict the future, but it's a good idea to have some expectations for how your relationship will develop when you live together. You can talk about the kind of dates you'd like to go on, whether it's a night at the movies or proving to your date that you're a mini golf champion once and for all.

You may better understand if your partner is introverted or extroverted in a home situation by having conversations, and you may begin to adjust expectations for a schedule that will work for both of you. Keep an open mind, but don't be afraid to share your thoughts on where you'd like to live or what names you might give your future dog.

Depending on how far along your relationship is, it is critical to discuss the prospect of having children or getting married to ensure that you and your partner are on the same page. These topics could be difficult to talk about from afar, but they're crucial ones that will have a long-term impact on your relationship.

You are aware that the goal line may shift or change entirely.

The day of the big move is one of the more memorable days in a long-distance relationship. When the long-distance portion of your relationship ends, there's almost always a move involved, whether it's you relocating closer to your partner, them relocating closer to you, or both of you moving to a new city together.

It's useful to remember that long-distance relationships might take months or years to come together, and a lot can happen during that time. Having a move-in date makes the ultimate goal of your time apart seem more attainable, but try to incorporate flexibility into your and your partner's schedules as well. If they deserve a promotion that would allow them to work longer distances, you should both discuss what you think should happen next.

Accept the things you can't control and accept the fact that you'll never know exactly what will happen in the future.

This will help you not only as a long-distance couple but also as a long-term relationship.

In all honesty, the people in a relationship are the only ones who fully know where it stands. Long-distance travel is challenging, but it is also extremely possible. In the end, small successes add up. You can get to the end if you put in the work, celebrate your partner's triumphs, and listen to them share about their good and bad days.

HOW TO HANDLE YOUR FIRST TIME IN A LONG DISTANCE RELATIONSHIP

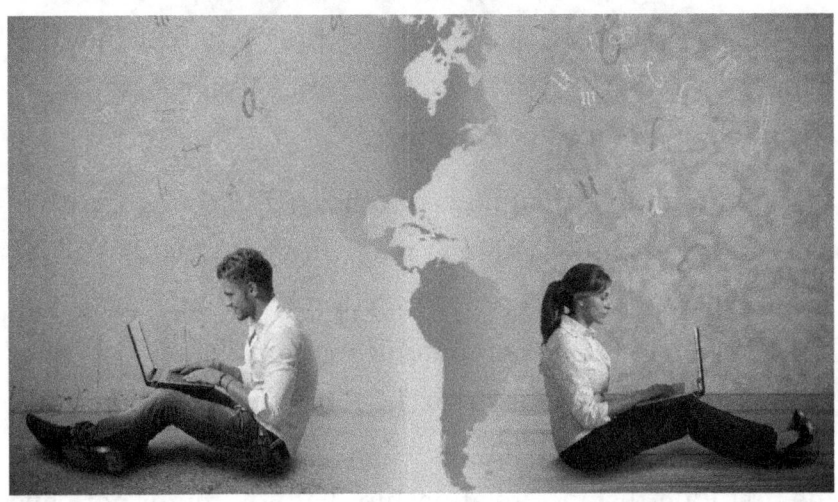

You might find yourself in an LDR at some point. Of course, this can happen in various ways: you meet someone while out of town, you meet someone in town, but one of you travels away for school or work, or there are a variety of different reasons you get yourself in an LDR. Some people learn the hard way, while others learn via trial and error. After all, few people intend to be in a long-distance relationship, so any guidance on doing so is beneficial. LDRs are undoubtedly possible in any event, but the more information you have beforehand, the better.

Dr. Suzana Flores, clinical psychologist and also the author of Facehooked: According to Bustle, Facebook has an impact on our emotions, relationships, and lives. "Distance between you and your lover can complicate your relationship, but if you keep a few things in mind, it can work out. Additionally, keep in mind that distance makes the heart grow fonder. The beautiful thing about long-distance relationships is that even the simplest things - like spending time together, holding hands, or going out for coffee - can become even more significant when you are together."

When you and your significant other get back together, it's true that the simplest things may turn into big moments. Meanwhile, when you're separated, many things are given in LDRs, such as good communication and trust, but other things aren't as obvious in the LDR rule book. Relationship experts weigh in on what you should know before starting the first long-distance relationship that you might not have considered.

Agree On Expectations

Isn't it the worst when you and your lover don't communicate? When you add in some distance and the fact that they aren't readily available for a face-to-face talk, miscommunications might become much more exaggerated. As a result, Dr. Flores recommends talking about your expectations. "Sit down with your partner and then discuss what you expect from one other while you are away before you decide to be involved in a long-distance relationship," she advises. "Decide the relationship's 'rules.' Will you both date other individuals or stick to each other? Although such discussions might be painful, they are vital to avoid being caught off guard by assumptions and misunderstandings."

Setting expectations is also vital, according to Terrie Lewine, relationship and communication coach and founder of BACK TO LIFE Urban Sanctuary, who has been in a long-distance relationship for 17 years. She tells Bustle, "Build trust with well-thought-out agreements." "How frequently do you expect to speak? What is your plan for seeing each other? Who goes on vacation? "Who is responsible for what?" She also emphasizes the importance of speaking out if you wish to adjust the expectations you and your spouse have established. "If you recognize that you are unhappy, contact your partner right away and attempt to renegotiate. The more open you are about the benefits (and challenges) of a long-distance relationship, and the more honest you are about how to negotiate them, the more likely you will enjoy your time together and apart. If you can't appreciate the time apart, then a long-distance relationship isn't for you."

Maintain Consistency, Especially When It Comes to Communication

Even though you already know how crucial communication is in a relationship, especially long-distance, you must also ensure that it is consistent. "In long-distance relationships, consistency is incredibly helpful," Sameera Sullivan, Founder of Lasting Connections, tells Bustle. "Find a period that works for both of your schedules to communicate –

chatting before the night is a good time to strive for because the chat will be less rushed and will summarize the entire day." Texting, phoning, FaceTiming, voice notes, snap chatting, Google Hangouts, and other methods of communication are also suggested by Sullivan. "Make a point of it to stay in touch and have fun with it – none of this should feel like a chore! If it does, something isn't quite right, and you should consider why."

Sullivan also recommends keeping your partner informed about your plans to minimize wounded feelings and unreasonable expectations. She advises, "Let the other person know, so they aren't concerned or anxious when they don't hear from you." "Doing so gives you the chance to make someone you care about feel included in your life, which is always a good thing."

Keep a safe distance.

Even though you're already coping with distance in an LDR, that doesn't mean you have to communicate all the time. After all, you want to maintain a healthy level of communication, not burn it out by talking too much. "You might still need some distance," Dr. Flores advises, despite the distance. "You may feel compelled to communicate more frequently to compensate for the distance between you and your companion. However, if you communicate too much, the relationship may appear to be burdensome. It's perfectly acceptable to miss your mate. Otherwise, you might both feel stressed and fatigued trying to keep the relationship going."

To each other, be kind and truthful.

Stay committed once you've established that you and your long-distance spouse are on the same commitment level. In this vein, Antonia Hall, a psychologist, relationship specialist, and author of the Sexy Little Guide books, emphasizes the need to trust each other and not act in ways that can jeopardize that trust. She tells Bustle, "You have to be able to trust the individual; otherwise, it won't be a nice, healthy experience." "It's better to ask questions than to go off on a tangent... Behaving graciously and compassionately demonstrates that you are trustworthy and caring, and your significant other will ideally reciprocate."

Don't shy away from conflict.

Communication is essential in every relationship, whether long-distance or not. However, interacting with the latter may be more difficult, making it all the more crucial. According to Grant Langston, CEO of eHarmony, "some couples in LDRs forgo the ordinary chat and get to more important things." "However, by chatting about everything that happens throughout your day, you are reproducing a circumstance that most geographically close couples would find themselves in, and you will learn more about your partner. Because they don't have the time to resolve disagreements, LDR couples tend to avoid them in their interactions. Conflict, on the other hand, can be beneficial in that it allows you to learn how your spouse handles stressful situations in their lives and allows you to work on particular areas before reconciling permanently."

When you're not with your partner, learn more about yourself.

Although it is a given that while you are in an LDR, you will have more "me" time, the goal is to make the most of it. Shannon Smith, the resident dating expert, tells Bustle, "Perhaps the most crucial thing you need to know when going into a long-distance relationship is that your existing relationship with yourself will become very evident, very fast." "When you find yourself with a lot of time on your hands, put it to good use! Invest in your personal development and self-care! You'll be a better partner if you're your greatest self — and your relationship with yourself will last a lifetime!"

It's possible that not every trip will be fantastic.

Even if you eagerly anticipate meeting your long-distance lover, reality may not always meet your expectations, and that's fine. Breakup coach, advice columnist, and host of the podcast Thank You Heartbreak Chelsea Leigh Trescott of Breakupward.com agrees. She tells Bustle, "Not every journey to see each other is going to live up to your aspirations and dreams." "In order to weather what could feel like a letdown when it comes to parting ways again, you'll need to build a stunning degree of realism, fortitude, perspective, and patience. Make sure you don't fall for the all-or-nothing mentality." If the vacation does not go as planned, Trescott advises not to think the relationship is doomed.

"Just because the trip wasn't great doesn't imply you don't matter to your partner now," she explains. "Believe in yourself and your relationship," says the author. And keep in mind that a single disagreement or an off day together shouldn't be enough to build or end a healthy relationship."

Create an LDR budget.

LDRs may be as romantic as they are expensive. You could wish to start an LDR budget, whether it's a jar in your room for spare change or a bank account you open. Margaux Cassuto, a relationship expert and matchmaker at Three Matches who was also in a long-distance relationship with her now-husband, tells Bustle that having a flexible schedule as well as money to spend on vacation is crucial.

Trescott agrees that money is a component of LDRs that you might not consider at first but should. "The truth that your money will need to be in place is sometimes an omission when it comes to long-distance relationships," she says. Even though there are numerous ongoing fees associated with in-city relationships, Trescott claims that these expenditures are spread out over time more so than the cost of a plane ticket.

"You'll need to not burn out your funds early on attempting to placate each other with expensive efforts if you want the relationship to have the best chance of lasting on a logistical level," she advises.

Keep in mind that your partner has a life you may or may not be a part of.

Even if you and your long-distance partner feel linked, you will still live different lives. Laurel House, dating expert and resident sex expert for My First Blush, tells Bustle, "Be conscious that your person has a life outside of you where they live." "In other words, it's not like living in the same place and seeing each other all the time. Instead, they'll be spending their time with their friends and family, who have nothing to do with you," House adds. You can also miss out on certain things in your own city if you visit theirs, and vice versa.

She admits that LDRs can be a sacrifice. "You will also lose out on activities in your city because you are traveling to be with them, and they will lose out on things as well when they go to be with you."

Maintain a realistic perspective rather than a romantic one.

You know how you know you should break up with someone, but then you start thinking about all the nice moments you've had together, forgetting that you've had more *bad* times together than good? When it comes to LDRs, you must be pragmatic rather than ideological. "Some couples tend to romanticize their relationship and remember it as better than it was," says Langston. "Research has revealed that couples who are more idealized in their relationship are more likely to break up because their relationship is unstable. This might happen when you imagine your lover to be better than they are in your thoughts, resulting in an unpleasant reunion. You may feel as if you're reuniting with a whole stranger rather than someone you know and understand."

Langston offers a simple answer to the problem of idealizing your lover. "The greatest method to get to know someone and discover the reality of your relationship status is to spend quality time together and engage in person," he says. "A study found that spending more face-to-face time with a long-distance spouse reduces the likelihood of idealizing your partner. As a result, there'd be less likelihood of instability in your reunion."

Be adaptable.

Catherine Silver, LCSW, a psychotherapist in New York City, works with people in LDRs but in one for three years with her husband before they married. She tells Bustle, "LDRs are HARD." "They take time and effort, and while they can be rewarding, make sure you walk in with your eyes wide open. Any relationship requires commitment, but this one will require a greater level of devotion. Because a long-distance relationship is inconvenient, both sides must be committed to making it work. Find activities that you could do together, such as reading the same book or watching the same show."

She advises that while you should schedule certain activities together, you should also be flexible. "Things don't always go as planned, so being able to go with the flow is important."

Make sure you've got a game plan in place.

It's helpful to have a sense of when you'll be together again, not just in the short term but also in the long term, no matter where you are in an LDR — shortly before it starts or several weeks or months in. "In the early stages of an LDR, both partners must discuss their game plan," Amie Leadingham, Amie, the Dating Coach, tells Bustle. "If they're or were to fall in love, what would happen next? How will the LDR become an in-person relationship in the future?"

As you can see, there are some things you should be aware of before embarking on your first long-distance relationship. However, the information presented above will undoubtedly assist you in achieving the best LDR possible.

TRIED AND TRUE TIPS FOR YOUR LDR

Absence, it seems, really makes the heart grow fonder.

People in long-distance relationships are more likely to share meaningful ideas and feelings with their partners. Couples in long-distance relationships appear to idealize their partners' behaviors, resulting in a heightened sense of intimacy.

That is all well and good, but even for couples with a solid foundation, being away can be challenging at times. What are your set down strategies for getting through it? People who have struggled with long-distance relationships give their tried-and-true tips below.

Tip 1: Expect to put in twice as much effort as you did previously.

"During college, my now-husband, the then-boyfriend, went to school full-time in Utah, while I stayed home and finished high school before enrolling in a local college. We knew our relationship was worth fighting for, even though we were young, and we were determined to get through those years. We've now been married for five years and have been together for a total of 12 years. One thing we've discovered? When you're long-distance, you need to work on building a strong, stable foundation for your relationship. Be trustworthy, upfront, and honest. Take the time to choose how and when you should interact with one another. Even if you don't see each other, try to make each other feel special. In a long-distance relationship, everything you work on in a stable relationship will require extra effort." Alexandra Starkovich, blogger at My Urban Family

Tip 2: Make some ground rules for when you and your partner will see each other.

"My husband and I worked and went to school long distance for a total of five and a half years, with me working and going to school in Toronto and him in Florida. We established a rule that we couldn't go more than six weeks without seeing each other, and we pretty much followed it. We were still living apart when we married, and my green card took a year to arrive after we were married, following which I relocated to the United States in 2013." Allison Bowsher, freelance writer

Tip 3: Keep in touch with each other throughout the day by calling and texting.

"In our relationship, my wife and I have had to travel significant distances twice. When we initially met, she was in San Jose, approximately an hour away, and I was in San Francisco. After we married, I worked in San Francisco and she in Los Angeles, and we barely saw each other a few times a month. It's been discovered that you must phone and text each other throughout the day to keep in touch and explain what's going on. To put it another way, don't put it off till the end of the day when you're weary. Matty Staudt, writer and general manager of Urban Knights Radio, says, "Make your relationship a part of your daily life."

Tip 4: Remember to set up regular Skype dates.

"It's critical that you and your partner establish a communication routine. Although we are lucky to have access to so many various communication methods these days, texting alone is insufficient to maintain a long-distance relationship. To keep a solid relationship, you should communicate on the phone as much as possible, preferably using a program like Skype! " Anna Genevieve Louise, The Wanderlust Collective blogger

Tip #5: Take a step back and consider the broad picture.

"In the broader scheme of things, this was critical. My partner and I met at university and had been dating for around 3 1/2 years before leaving Nigeria to pursue his master's degree in the United Kingdom. In the year 2011, for approximately two years, we were separated. We had to keep reminding ourselves that the distance was only temporary and that we had to make it work because we really wanted to be together. This helps put things in perspective and navigate through any challenges. It also aided our future plans, as I became more inclined to contemplate the United Kingdom. Kachi Tila-Adesina, blogger at Kachee Tee: "For my own master's program, so that we could be together."

Tip #6: Make a big deal out of everything.

"In college, my spouse and I had known one other. We started dating after he joined the Navy. We were a couple of states away at the time. He was sent overseas for a year shortly after we got engaged. We discovered that you should celebrate everything, even if you can't be together in person. Life is far too short not to, especially when you're in a long-distance relationship." Jo, blogger @ Jo, My Gosh! Modern Military Spouse: The Ultimate Military Life Guide for New Spouses and Significant Others is her co-authored book.

Tip #7: Get an airline-miles-earning credit card.

"I was in New York City, and my husband Matt was at Miami Beach," she explained. We had a two-year commuter relationship. With the help of my American Express card, I was able to acquire free flights virtually every other month. Pick a card with an airline component to maximize your points." Emily Nolan, model and blogger at My Kind of Life

Tip 8: Don't be concerned if your visits aren't perfect.

"When it comes to long-distance relationships, there's a lot of strain on trips. Do you like to socialize with your partner and friends or stay at home for one-on-one time? Is it possible for your family to spend time with your partner? Is it necessary for one of you to work or study during your visit? Is there a huge conversation looming in the background like the elephant in the room, and do you talk about it face to face when you have limited time together, or do you talk about it later over the phone? Some visits will be full of wonderful memories and happy times, while others may be full of squabbling over minor matters, and that's perfectly fine! Long-distance partnerships, like any 'real' relationships, have their ups and downs." Allison Bowsher

"I DON'T KNOW WHAT WE CAN TALK ABOUT ANYMORE"

Hearing from people in long-distance relationships all the time is a source of worry and concern. The distance can be intimidating, especially if you're in a new relationship or if your relationship is under duress (such as during a deployment) (like during a deployment).

Fun Questions to Ask Your Partner When You are in an LDR

Learning fresh things about each other, asking each other silly questions, and sharing as much of life with each other as possible adds spice to the mix. And those abilities that shared interest in one other would help you cope with the year-long separation when you wouldn't be able to see each other on weekends or communicate as much as you wanted.

Still, you might sometimes run out of things to talk about, or you revert to some of the same old, same old topics. If you're ready to freshen up your long-distance game, here are 99 fun questions to ask your partner!

1. What food do you wish you cook like a world-class chef?

2. What was the last book you read and really enjoyed? (Not sure? Check out these book suggestions for long-distance couples.)

3. What is one song that can always pull you out of a bad mood?

4. What is the most dreadful film you've ever seen?

5. Which celebrity do you think would be your best friend if you ever met?

6. What is the longest time you have ever gone without sleeping?

7. ...without taking a shower?

8. ...without a clean pair of underwear?

9. What is your most irritating pet peeve?

10. What is one superpower you would despise if you had?

11. What was something you misinterpreted as a kid and only later realized was incorrect?

12. What'd you change your name to if you had to?

13. Which color do you identify with the most?

14. What are your thoughts on horoscopes and astrology?

15. What holiday would you design if you were in charge?

16. Which fast food joint are you embarrassed to admit you enjoy?

17. What was the oddest thing you ever did when you were a kid?

18. What's the most amusingly misheard lyric you've ever heard?

19. What would you put in a time capsule if you could?

20. Which sports team would you rename, and how would you do it?

21. Have you ever performed on a stage?

22. Which game show do you think you'd have a good chance of winning?

23. Is there a game that you'd like to try that we haven't yet?

24. What do you consider to be your most egregious flaw?

25. ...what is your best quality?

26. Is it possible for you to define your ideal vacation?

27. What is something that makes you nervous?

28. What is your ideal brunch menu?

29. What is the name of your Patronus?

30. Which sandwich topping do you relate to the most?

31. What is one food from your childhood that you can't believe you ate?

32. What commercial irritates you the most?

33. What would you run for if you had to run for public office?

34. What are one or two aspects about the generation after you that you don't understand?

35. What are one or two aspects about the generation before you that you don't understand?

36. Which sport would you choose if you could only watch one sport for the rest of your life and all others were banned?

37. What are your thoughts on non-cucumber pickled foods?

38. Can you think of one issue that you know is ludicrous but about which you are adamant and will argue to the death?

39. Is there a flower or plant that you adore?

40. What kind of animal would you like to have as a pet?

41. Do you like to spend or preserve your money?

42. When you were a child, what did you wish to be when you grew up?

43. Do you prefer the mountains or the beach?

44. What has been the oddest dream you've ever had?

45. Would you consider getting a tattoo? Alternatively, what are your plans for your future tattoo?

46. Which celebrity chef would you most like to study under?

47. Is there anything you could do to lessen your stress?

48. What are your top three color choices?

49. Is there anything in your closet that you can't live without?

50. What have you tried that you thought you would despise but ended up enjoying?

51. Which emoji is your personal favorite?

52. What's the silliest knock-knock joke you've ever heard?

53. Which do you prefer: a dog, a cat, a fish, or a bird?

54. What kind of art would you make if you could become a master artist?

55. Which country would you like to travel to as a couple?

56. What do you think I should wear the most?

57. What's your favorite ice cream sundae topping?

58. What kind of piercings do you want?

59. What is your favorite time of year?

60. Which seasoning is your personal favorite?

61. What is your ideal automobile?

62. Did you have a favorite toy as a kid?

63. Do you have a favorite type of macaroni and cheese noodle?

64. What is one accomplishment of yours that you are really proud of?

65. Which of the following desserts is your personal favorite?

66. Which day of your life would you like to relive if you could?

67. Would you prefer to have photographs or paintings on the walls of your home or apartment?

68. Have you ever been the winner of a television or radio contest? What did you win if you did?

69. What is your favorite social networking platform?

70. ...which is your least favorite?

71. Which season is your favorite and why?

72. Which show, The Today Show, Good Morning America, or CBS This Morning, would you rather watch?

73. Which spa treatment is your personal favorite? What kind of spa treatment do you wish to try the most?

74. Is it better for people to unwrap gifts slowly or quickly?

75. What is your biggest gripe with the country?

76. What one item do you believe would strengthen our bond?

77. Do you have any festivals or activities in mind for the next time we get together?

78. What is your favorite aspect of a circus?

79. Which amusement park ride would be your first choice?

80. On a typical day, what type of beverage do you consume the most?

81. Which one of your skills would you wish to study or improve?

82. Which of the following are your top five snack foods?

83. Would you prefer to read the book first and then watch the movie, or would you watch the movie first before reading the book?

84. What's the latest comedy special you've seen?

85. Is there a show that you can't get enough of?

86. What are your thoughts on blending Play-Doh colors?

87. What's the longest you've ever gone without washing a pair of jeans?

88. What's your favorite underwear style?

89. When you were younger, what was your favorite fairy tale?

90. What occasion did you dress up in the most expensive clothes you've ever owned?

91. Who would you pick to meet if you could meet one person today, living or dead?

92. What song does it take to make you feel all the feels when you hear it on the radio?

93. What is your favorite holiday?

94. What do you consider to be your most valuable possession?

95. Do you prefer a crossword puzzle, a word search, or a sudoku puzzle?

96. What is a project that you would like to complete with your own two hands?

97. What is one widely accepted concept that you refuse to believe?

98. What is the most revolting fashion trend you've ever seen?

99. When we next encounter each other, what's the first thing you're going to do?

Dos and Don'ts When It Comes to Falling in Love and Long-Distance Dating

It isn't merely a question of communication.

It could be difficult to date someone from the same city. If you're not careful, dating someone from another country can be nearly impossible. Long-distance dating isn't as difficult as many people believe, and while the official success rates are a little hazy, we're confident you'll be able to make it work if you find yourself in this situation. Communication is important in any relationship, but it may not be the most vital aspect of a long-distance relationship's success.

We asked three partners who have been involved in cross-country relationships the two dos and don'ts of cross-country dating. We talked about everything from conversation to timings and what it takes to be clear. Read their stories of love and cross-country dating, as well as our two dos and don'ts for keeping the relationship strong and alive.

DO make sure that when it comes to a lengthy run, make sure you're inside it.

It can be frightening to consider how long your relationship will last. While you may be able to dismiss the matter in a regular relationship, you must discuss it with your spouse from the beginning of a long-distance relationship.

"Long term" might be the title of the game. Cross-country relationships progress in a different way than regular ones. Longer gaming is for a meaningful relationship with someone who will one day be your partner," says Andrea Miranda (29) of New York, who was recently in a long-distance relationship with her partner Richie (30) of Sevilla, Spain.

DO NOT Over Communicate

Jillian, a celebrity who lives in New York City while her partner Nina works as an instructor in Sarasota, Florida, believes that excessive engagement is a major issue.

"You spend a lot of time connected, but it becomes an obsessive interaction. Getting a sense of stability and assuring the quality of talks could be the task. We must arrive at the room when we are in need, as this is different from a check-in call. We need to be in touch."

DO Make sure that you have the same communication style.

One was in Orlando, Florida, and the other was in Brooklyn, New York, Charles (31) and his boyfriend Zach (28) were dating across the country. Before jumping into the partnership, Charles and Zach discussed their interaction designs:

"It had been critical to keeping in touch. His and my interface designs were practically identical. I've always believed that in cross-country relationships, you don't really have anything. if you do not have a good working relationship."

DO NOT rely on social media marketing.

"Do not be a social media outlet. We've all been in that situation. Regardless, it will drive you mad since you will either not receive any/enough information about them, or you will manufacture a complete problem in your head that is not an actual one. It may have worked when you were younger to make them envious by releasing scandalous images, stories, and so on, but the great news is now it only appears unfortunate," Andrea says.

"We believe we have now discovered that people require transparency. The more transparent we have been with the other person, the more connected we will feel. The importance of correspondence cannot be overstated. However, you must be receptive to keep up with the text. You should be prepared to say, "We have always felt right that is unhappy and lacking you." We feel closer when weвTMre open and honest. The ability to support your lover's autonomy and be self-assured enough to be comfortable with them being social. When you give up on that, it breaks apart," Nina and Jillian said.

Do Make date nights a priority.

Preparing date nights is one tool you may use to keep your relationship active. Rather than just communicating daily or weekly, consider planning a weeknight out when you both watch the same movie or play an online multiplayer game.

According to Nina and Jillian, date nights come in a variety of shapes and sizes. "Dates include FaceTime as well as other tasks," they say. We play puzzles together, watch movies together, watch The Handmaid's Tale together, read to one another, and practice our languages together. Together, we also discovered a Thai-friendly globe geography website.

Both of us downloaded settlers of Catan to try out. In addition, we enjoy sharing bedtime and poetry stories.

DO NOT expect all things to fall into place according to your plans.

Once again, this is the person you could want to spend the rest of your life with, but for now, spend some time with. Although it is cheesy, the proper person will take the time to find a way to stay true to themselves," Andrea explains.

"The very best reason for our relationship is the fact that there is simply no endgame," Nina and Jillian said. We've talked about weddings and cohabitation, but we're completely self-contained in our daily lives. On our endgame, we go back and forth. Is it possible to have three places? We have recently highlighted Jillian's university education, and we will continue. There isn't any force. You want to let it happen on its own time. Our goal is usually to be together at the end of the day. "However, we aren't in a rush."

Do Make plans to go on a trip/vacation together.

Charles and Zach had a feeling they'd end up together from the start. Instead, they are introduced through a common acquaintance and do not begin dating for several years. But, according to Charles, they may frequently visit each other:

"We could chat for the rest of the day. There was certainly no time when no one was speaking. Fortunately, I worked from home and was able to visit New York anytime I wanted. We'd see each other every couple of weeks or so."

Andrea and Richie met in Sevilla, Spain, and stayed in touch when Andrea moved back to New York. Richie would go to Andrea, but it wasn't until Andrea moved back to Sevilla that Richie ultimately made the decision:

"You'll have to make plans to see each other. Because you may not be in each other's day-to-day lives, you'll need to make sure you see each other and spend time together. I enjoy traveling somewhere new with my partner to create new memories and share new experiences. This may also clear out people who aren't interested in you; trust me when I say they won't make plans. " Andrea claims.

DO NOT *Forget to establish appropriate boundaries.*

Relationships can be intensely passionate, but we must establish good boundaries from the beginning. There is nothing about letting your spouse know what's acceptable and what's not. Maybe not everything has to be grayscale, but connecting with your limitations is better to avoid problems later on.

"I can't text and call and text and call and text and call (well, at the least only a few some time in a hopeless means). If it is really too much, you will know and feel it. Let us be honest. " Andrea says.

HOW TO MAKE YOUR LONG DISTANCE RELATIONSHIP WORK

You finally found someone worth holding onto after a long search. And you're in a great relationship. However, you may find yourself separated from the one you love by thousands of kilometers due to unforeseen circumstances.

Regardless of how much you love one other, a part of you is certainly wondering how or if your relationship will survive the distance between you.

You've recently started dating someone fantastic. You get along well, have a good time together, and everything appears to be going great. The only issue? They've just gotten a job offer in another state for their ideal job. Perhaps you connected with someone online who lives on the opposite side of the country.

Long-distance relationships can be terrifying and difficult, but they can and do work. They simply necessitate a little more thought and effort.

A lot of the same elements are required for local and long-distance relationships. Long-distance ones, on the other hand, will necessitate a little more thought.

According to Patrick Cheatham, PsyD, "people in long-distance relationships must be considerably more purposeful and hardworking in performing the work that helps partnerships thrive."

Long-distance relationships can undoubtedly succeed, so take comfort in that. Most couples, at some point throughout their dating or married relationship, find themselves geographically separated.

Many couples credit a period of long-distance communication as the foundation of a stronger relationship.

With this in mind, our team of relationship specialists at Lasting has put up a list of their best advice for maintaining, surviving, and even thriving in a long-distance relationship or marriage.

We hope it's only a matter of time before you and the one you love are back together. In the meantime, here are some therapist-approved suggestions for strengthening your emotional bond, easing the pain of geographic separation, and ensuring that your partnership lasts.

Examine your communication requirements.

Decide how often you want to talk when you first start a long-distance relationship, aside from occasional text messages throughout the day.

You may both agree that you want to chat a lot, but you may disagree about what that entails. Finding a compromise early on will help you avoid annoyance later on if your desired levels of communication differ.

A communication calendar can also be beneficial. This plan does not have to be rigid, but knowing when you'll hear from your partner next can be comforting.

A surprise phone call while you're both at your best might be wonderful, but scheduling longer discussions can help you connect when you're both at your best. If your companion is a night owl and you are a morning person, schedule calls right before or after dinner.

Keep your independence.

This is a significant issue. Keep in mind that you have a separate existence in your city. If your partner is thousands of miles away, you may feel like a piece of yourself is missing, but try to keep up with your typical activities. Furthermore, staying busy can assist in alleviating feelings of loneliness.

If you don't see your partner very often, you should talk to them more often. If they can't always talk to you, feeling tethered to your phone or computer might lead to unhappiness or even anger. You'll also miss out on time with those people you care about.

Even if your partner has plenty of time to converse throughout the day, it's still a good idea to spend some time alone or with friends and family.

When at all feasible, stick to your 'meeting' times.

Would you want to date someone who keeps missing in-person dates over an extended period?

Physical separation might make a partnership appear more casual. However, long-term relationships require you to prioritize your partner, just as you would while dating someone locally.

When things go wrong, a partner who is too far away to help may be more concerned than a local partner if they don't hear from you on time. Things may inevitably arise, but try to notify your partner as soon as possible. Also, if possible, set up a makeup consultation.

Change up your communication methods.

Changing up how you communicate could help you feel more connected. For example, you might use Snapchat to send photos and videos, Facebook Messenger to remain in touch, text occasionally, and make a brief phone call during your lunch break or when you get up in the morning.

It's worth noting that keeping track of several chats might be overwhelming for some people, so this method may not be suitable for everyone.

Consider using non-digital communication methods as well. For example, most people's days are brightened by receiving a letter or a surprise present.

Consider sharing a letter diary or scrapbook with notes, photos, and souvenirs from your daily life. Then, send it back and forth, adding to it as you go.

Make the most of your communication.

It's natural to feel like you never have enough time to chat with your partner in a long-distance relationship. If this sounds like you, concentrate your efforts on getting the most out of communication.

Make a list of things you want to share as you think of them during the day so you don't forget. If you have something in mind, speak up rather than keeping it to yourself.

...but don't forget the mundane.

You may not feel physically close to your lover due to distance. Minor nuances, on the other hand, can make you feel even more emotionally distant.

Your inclination may prompt you to concentrate on profound or meaningful issues to maximize the value of the discussions you do have. Things that don't matter in the larger scheme of things, on the other hand, can help you develop a positive image of your partner and strengthen your emotional bond.

So vent or ramble to one other, and don't be afraid to disclose seemingly insignificant, even mundane details like what you ate for breakfast, your new neighbors, or how you stepped in cat puke on the restroom floor. After all, you'd probably tell a spouse you see every day about such things.

Don't overlook closeness.

In many long-distance relationships, maintaining sexual closeness is a major difficulty. If you and your spouse have regular intercourse, the absence of intimate contact during your weeks (or months) apart may be a source of frustration.

Even if you're separated, you can still connect deeply.

Intimacy from afar

To keep things fresh, try:

- sending romantic emails, letters, or texts
- sharing sexual photos (but make sure your messaging program is safe)
- talking about sex and things you'd like to try
- phone sex
- mutual masturbation during a video chat

Remember that not everyone is comfortable with digital intimacy, so always talk about personal limits regarding photos, phone sex, or webcam use.

It's natural to feel timid or embarrassed at first, but don't be afraid to express these feelings. Sharing unpleasant times can really aid in the development of greater connection.

Exchange physical mementos of one another.

The items of a loved one can hold a lot of sentimental value for you.

Consider their toothbrush in the bathroom, their favorite jam in the fridge, or even the shampoo aroma on the bed pillows. All of these things can help you remember your partner's presence even if they're thousands of miles away.

Consider leaving some of your stuff with each other on your next visit. For example, hang some clothing in the closet, put some books on the shelf, and pick up a favorite brand of tea or coffee to take with you.

Those items will be waiting for you the next time you visit. But, in the interim, they might make you both feel that the period between visits isn't as long as it appears.

When possible, spend time together.

Time, money, and work obligations can make it tough to see your spouse as frequently as you'd want.

Consider doing some advance planning to secure a good bargain on aircraft tickets or look into other modes of transportation, like trains or ride-sharing.

You might also try mixing things up by meeting midway to lighten the load.

To feel connected, communicate as much (or as little) as you need.

We are living in an era where we have unrivaled 24-hour access to one another. So devoting a significant amount of free time to catching up with a long-distance partner may be a wonderful gift — as long as you and your partner are on the same page about it.

Some couples desire to feel linked at all times. On the other hand, some people find it exhausting to converse every day. Talk about what works best for you in terms of the general frequency and length of time you'll spend texting, calling, or video conferencing each day or week. Also, be willing to change your communication habits as life throws you new and unexpected challenges.

Even if you can't physically be there, "be there."

According to decades of research, the happiest relationships are those in which one partner properly responds to the emotional needs of the other. Thousands of modest attempts to communicate with each other are referred to as emotional calls. One of the themes covered in detail in Lasting's marriage health session is the premier relationship health app.

You're really asking each other one question at the heart of every emotional call:

"Are you going to be there for me?" "

In a long-distance relationship, responding to each other's emotional calls might be difficult. You can not physically show up for each other's important days or give a hug to reassure someone. This isn't to say that this vital aspect of relationship success isn't significant.

Long-distance couples may instead need to be more deliberate in their responses to each other's attempts to connect. If you've set aside time to communicate with your spouse, treat the call as if it were a work meeting or a doctor's appointment. If your partner has a big day coming up, call or text ahead of time to see how it went. By incorporating your partner's demands into your daily routine, you'll show that you care about them, no matter how far away you are.

Remind your partner of the stuff you enjoy about your relationship regularly.

Long-distance relationships can be fraught with doubts, fears, and envy because you spend so much time apart. This is why the therapists advocate giving each other frequent verbal affirmations. They aid in the reduction of bad feelings and the clarification of your relationship's position.

Tell your sweetheart how much you love and cherish your relationship the next time you communicate. And if you are not sure about your position, don't hesitate to seek reassurance for yourself. It is as lovely to say as it is to hear, "I love you and wish we could be together today."

Form a strong bond by supporting each other's goals.

You and your partner would continue to grow and evolve as life goes on, whether you're together or apart. That is both normal and beneficial, even if it requires some changes in your relationship.

According to therapists, long-distance coupleswhot have a stable relationship can allow each other to grow and progress. They find methods to stay in touch and encourage one another. Personal growth and change are good in a solid attachment connection. Again, it's a result of the relationship's stability and safety.

Supporting your partner as they develop their particular abilities and interests is one of the best things you can do to promote a stable bond. While it may be aggravating if her new volleyball practice interferes with your nightly catch-up time, it's critical to encourage her to pursue her passions, just as she should for you.

Find a way to stay in touch when you're away.

According to research, interdependent relationships are the healthiest type of married partnership. But, what exactly does that imply? That is, you and your spouse accomplish things in unison while keeping separate identities as individuals. Your long-distance circumstances are probably driving you to do more things individually than you'd want, which is why it's critical to select a few activities you can accomplish together remotely.

Sharing experiences with your long-distance partner, according to marriage therapist Liz Colizza, strengthens your bond. "Finding activities you can do as a couple to make you feel more connected pays off big time. When it seems as though the distance is pulling you in two opposite directions, that's a major win."

Reading the same book, watching the same show on Netflix while talking on the phone. Playing online games, listening to the same playlist, or even eating at the same chain restaurant on the same night can all help you and your partner feel more interdependent and, ultimately, more connected.

Learn how to deal with pressing situations both online and in person.

Whether you live in the same house or across the ocean, all couples must develop healthy ways to discuss and resolve issues. If you dismiss little issues or refuse to discuss sensitive matters, you may face bigger ones.

This happened to one military spouse when she and her husband were dating long distances. "I've never felt at ease discussing sensitive topics over the phone. But I did not want to spoil our time together by creating an argument when I went to see him. It created a vicious loop in which I felt unable to express what was bothering me. I was going to blow out and break up with him eventually. It was particularly unjust because he had no notion anything was wrong."

If you're having trouble bringing up uncomfortable issues, pairing the Lasting app with them will help you ease into them. Through Talkspace, you can also obtain more personalized help from a therapist.

It takes time and effort to learn how to communicate about difficult matters, but it's critical to the health of your long-distance relationship that you don't let tiny issues turn into large ones.

Concentrate on the advantages of long-distance travel.

Being apart from the person you adore can hardly be described as a good thing. However, where you can not change your circumstances right away, you can change your mindset right away.

One of Lasting's users explained how he learned to value his long-distance status. "It may sound strange, but I enjoyed being in a long-distance relationship. When we were together, I could give my girlfriend my undivided attention. When we were separated, I concentrated on my studies and social activities. While I was in law school, that worked incredibly well for us."

Try to think of a few methods through which your long-distance relationship is actually advantageous, as frustrating as it may appear. For example, do you have extra time for hobbies, exercise, or socializing with friends and family? Make a list of the advantages of running long distances and concentrate on them on the days when the distance is getting to you.

Respect each other's reasons for being apart.

There will undoubtedly be days when your long-distance relationship appears particularly challenging. You may even be tempted to do something rash, such as quitting your job or dropping out of school, just to be with the person you love.

While that may sound romantic, keep in mind that there's a reason you're now separated from the person you love. That reason could be related to a professional, financial, or family circumstance that needs to be resolved until the time is perfect for you both to be geographically together.

Don't allow months or years of hard work to go to waste because you're eager to be together. If you finish what you have started and finish it well, your connection will be stronger in the long run.

Make a long-term plan for integrating your worlds when the time is appropriate.

Anyone who has been in a long-distance relationship knows how heartbreaking it is to be apart from the person you love. If you are in a relationship with the person you want to spend the rest of your life with, you'll need to devise a strategy for bringing your worlds together at some time.

Make sure your plan considers the proper next move at the proper time for both individuals, whether it's a wedding, an engagement, a work shift, or a relocation.

Having the hope of remaining together, in the long run, can help you get through the most difficult days apart. That sliver of hope can go a long way toward making the person you care about feel closer.

Avoid excessive communication.

Being extremely "sticky" and possessive is not a good idea. You don't have to talk for 12 hours a day to keep your relationship going. Many couples believe that doing more will compensate for the distance. This isn't correct. And it may make things worse. You'd get tired of "loving" in no time.

Keep in mind that little is more. It's not about spamming; you'll only tire yourself that way. It's all about teasing and tugging at the appropriate times and in the correct places.

Consider it an opportunity.

"Learning to live apart is the first step toward living together." – Anonymous

Consider it a learning experience for both of you. Consider it a test of your love for one another. "Real gold does not fear the test of fire," as the Chinese proverb says. So instead of thinking that your long-distance relationship is dragging you apart, you should trust that this experience will strengthen your bond even more.

In season four of Glee, Emma tells Will,

"I'd rather be here, far away from you but feeling very close, than close to you but feeling very far away." – Emma, Season 4 of Glee

To keep your expectations in check, establish some ground rules.

During this long-distance relationship, both of you must be clear about what you expect of one other. Set some ground rules so neither of you'd do something that will surprise the other.

Are you two, for example, exclusive? Is it okay if the other person goes on dates with you? What is your degree of commitment? It's preferable to be honest with one another about all of these issues.

Make an effort to communicate frequently and creatively.

Every day, greet each other with "good morning" and "good night" greetings. Additionally, try to keep your partner up to date on your life and events, no matter how mundane some of them might seem.

Send each other pictures, audio clips, and short videos from time to time to up the ante. You make the next person feel loved and cared for when you put in this kind of effort.

Make filthy jokes at each other.

One of the most significant areas of a relationship is sexual tension. Sexual desire acts as a glue that holds both partners together and prevents them from drifting away. Thus, not only is sex a physical requirement, but it is also an emotional one.

Send each other tempting texts full of sexual innuendos and suggestive descriptions to keep the fires burning. Sexy puns are also effective.

Stay away from "dangerous" circumstances.

If you are already aware that going to the club or drinking late at night with your pals will irritate your partner, you should either

1. Do not do it; alternatively

2. Tell your partner ahead of time to reassure them.

Don't be careless about this since you're placing your spouse in a position where they feel weak or in control, which will only make them more apprehensive or suspicious and, of course, very upset.

It might also be simple for you to slip into the trap you build for yourself by "meeting up" with your office eye-candy after the close of work or going out with someone from your past who's been flirting with you, whether consciously or unconsciously. Before you approach the situation, you must first recognize the threats.

Don't only follow your heart's lead. Pay attention to your thoughts as well.

Collaborate on projects.

Play an online game with your friends. Simultaneously, watch a documentary on YouTube or Vimeo. Then, on Skype, sing to each other as one of you plays the guitar. Outside, while video-calling each other, "take a walk together." Finally, go online shopping with each other and buy gifts for each other.

Carry out identical actions.

Recommend books, TV series, movies, music, current events, and other items. You have more common ground to discuss when you read, watch, and listen to the same things.

Even though you live apart, this is a terrific way to establish some shared experiences.

Pay each other a visit.

Every long-distance relationship revolves upon visits.

After all the waiting, wanting, and abstinence, you finally get to meet one other to fulfill the little things like kissing, holding hands, and so on, which are all common to other couples but particularly meaningful and intimate for those in long-distance relationships.

Fireworks, glitter bombs, confetti, rainbows, and butterflies will be thrown everywhere.

Make a goal for yourself.

"At the end of the day, what do we want to accomplish?" " "How long do you think we'll be apart? "How do you feel about the future? " These are the questions you and your partner should be asking themselves.

The reality is that no pair can maintain a long-distance relationship indefinitely. So we'll all have to settle down at some point.

So develop a plan with your friends. Make a timeline with the estimated times apart and times together, as well as a final goal.

You and your partner must be on the same page and share the same objectives. So that, even if you don't share the same location or timezone, you're both motivated to work together in the same direction toward a future that involves both of you.

You do, after all, need the drive to keep a relationship going.

Take advantage of your alone time as well as your time with friends and family.

You may be alone, but you are not lonely unless you choose to be. You don't have to allow your partner's life to revolve around them; you still have yourself, your friends, and your family. Take advantage of this time to spend more time with your friends and family. Make it a habit to go to the gym regularly. Find a new pastime. Binge-watch your favorite series. There are many activities you can do that do not require your partner's participation.

Maintain an open line of communication with one another.

Talk about your fears, insecurities, jealousy, indifference, and whatever else is on your mind. If you try to hide a secret from your partner, it will eventually consume you from the inside out. Do not try to handle everything on your own. Instead, communicate with one other openly and honestly. Allow your spouse to assist you and provide you with the support you require. It's preferable to address a problem when it's still in its early stages than to wait until it's too late.

You should be aware of each other's schedules.

Knowing when the other person is busy and when they are available is useful to send a text or call at the appropriate time. You don't want to wake up your spouse in the middle of a class or the middle of a work meeting. Know about the tiny and significant events in each other's lives, such as college midterms and examinations, crucial business trips and meetings, job interviews, and so on. This is very important if you and your partner live in separate time zones.

Keep an eye on each other's social media posts.

On Facebook and Instagram, they like each other's images. Send each other tweets. Tag one another. Exchange items for each other's walls. Demonstrate your concern. Keep your stalking to a minimum.

Give the other individual a sentimental item to hold on to.

A memento has a lot of power. Whether it's a little pendant, a ring, a keychain, a collection of songs and movies, or a bottle of perfume, there's something for everyone. We routinely ascribe significance to little objects and stuff in our daily lives, whether consciously or unconsciously. This is the thing we all do: we try to store memories in tangible objects in the hopes of looking at or holding on to something that will help us recall when our minds fail us. This is why something so basic may mean so much to someone, even if it is of little or no value to others.

Make sure you have a good messaging app.

This is critical because texting is the most regular and frequent mode of contact between you two. Therefore, you'll need a solid messaging program on mobile phones that allows for more than simply text and emoticons.

LINE is a chat program that I use personally. It's effective, in my opinion, because it includes a large library of amusing and really amusing "stickers" that users can use for free. You may also go to the app's "Sticker Shop" to get extra stickers of various themes (such as Hello Kitty, Pokemon, Snoopy, MARVEL, and so on) for a modest price. The app also offers out free sticker sets for certain campaigns from time to time. This messaging software is adorable and simple to use.

Send your gift via snail mail.

Postcards and handwritten love messages are sent to each other. From time to time, they send each other gifts across the globe. Birthdays, anniversaries, and Valentine's Day flower delivery Shop together online for fashionable T-shirts, attractive undergarments, and other items.

Maintain an optimistic attitude.

To keep alive a long-distance relationship, you must consistently infuse good energy into it. Yes, waiting can be hard and lonely at times, but you must remind yourself that the fruits will be as delicious as heaven in the end.

Being appreciative all of the time is a great way to stay positive. Be grateful that you have someone to adore and who loves you in return. Be grateful for the small things, such as the handwritten note that came in your mailbox safely the other day. Be grateful for one another's health and well-being.

Keep each other informed on the friends and family of each other.

Because the finest topics to talk about are usually gossip and scandals.

Whenever possible, make a video call.

Because looking into each other's eyes and hearing each other's voices can make everything better.

Makeup pet names for each other.

Because it's adorable, it maintains a romantic atmosphere.

LONG-DISTANCE ACTIVITIES FOR COUPLES

Walking through the grocery store, you spot a couple debating different peanut butter. You experience a stab of envy that they get to accomplish this tedious activity together.

But physical distance doesn't mean you can't accomplish things together, especially with contemporary technology. You'd just have to be a bit creative.

Watch a movie together

Thanks to the rise of streaming, you may view movies or TV shows on opposite sides of the world.

Synchronize the start of the movie by starting at exactly the same moment. For example, one spouse might alternatively view through the webcam while the other partner plays the movie, although this can make it tougher to see or hear (though this may not matter if you're watching "Goodfellas" for the hundredth time).

Enjoy the movie with your companion by calling or video chatting as you watch. Relax and be yourself, just like you would if your lover were in the room with you.

Go for a walk

Share a walk with your spouse by conversing on the phone while you spend time outside in your neighborhood, a favorite area, or somewhere altogether new. You can discuss any fresh or fascinating things you see and even take pictures.

If feasible, do this when they're on a stroll, too. Again, organizing the same activity at the same time can help you feel more connected.

While walking and video chatting simultaneously can be risky, choose a quiet area in your neighborhood to make a quick video call.

Take up a hobby as a couple.

Hobbies can test you, let you spend the time in a fun way, and help you relax. Consider finding something you and your partner can do together if you both have adequate time to try out a new pastime.

Look for a hobby you can undertake at home to video chat or communicate on speaker mode.

There are numerous options to think about:

- knitting
- woodwork
- sketch or painting
- baking
- cooking
- yoga
- attempting to learn a new language

You could even work on multiple projects at the same time. Video chatting as one of you practices guitar and the other draws, for example, can mimic the kind of evening you'd have if you were physically together.

Cook and eat dinner as a family.

If you and your partner both enjoy cooking together, continue the custom even when you're not together. Make the same recipe and see if it turns out the same way - just make sure your phone or computer isn't near any food or drink!

Make a date night out of it.

You may not be able to go on a date in person, but you may still create a romantic environment at home. Put on some music and toast with a glass of wine (or your favorite drink).

If you both do the following, the evening will feel more special.

- wear elegant clothes
- place candles on the table.
- prepare a meal that both of you will appreciate

Finish on a romantic note with a video call while bathing in a candlelit tub and having an intimate talk. Many partnerships require physical intimacy, and even if you can't be physically intimate, you may still generate intimacy and a sense of closeness.

Make it a point to include each other at family and friend gatherings.

If you and your partner usually visit each other's friends and family for social events, holidays, or other events, there's no reason you can't do so again via video chat.

Maintaining a sense of connection in each other's lives might be as simple as continuing to share special events or even informal hangouts. It also allows you to stay in touch with family and friends you might otherwise miss out on.

This type of communication is especially vital if one person lives alone in a new city with no family nearby. Just be sure that the rest of the group is aware that they will be hosting a virtual visitor.

Collaborate on household tasks.

The majority of individuals despise doing their tasks. Dishes, laundry, and toilet cleaning are probably not your favorite ways to spend an evening, especially if you have to do everything yourself.

While you can't help each other from hundreds of miles away, conversing while you can make activities seem less tedious.

This isn't going to work for everyone. It's unlikely that either of you wants to witness the other scrubbing the litter box or cleaning the drains. However, try going on a folding laundry date or chatting while cleaning out the fridge (they might even recall what's in that Tupperware you're terrified to open).

What to stay away from

Long-distance relationships, like any other type of connection, aren't a one-size-fits-all situation. What works for one marriage may not work for the next.

In any long-distance relationship, there are a few things you should generally avoid doing.

Keeping an eye on your partner

Long-distance relationships necessitate trust to keep your relationship's boundaries intact.

Of course, this is true in any relationship, but it can be crucial in one in which you have no means of knowing if your spouse is doing what they claim they're doing.

When your partner's conduct appears weird, it's natural to be concerned. They may miss a goodnight call for a few days, chat a lot about new pals, or appear less responsive to communications.

Instead of letting your worries mislead you into asking for confirmation of where they were or images of them in bed each night, convey your concerns.

Every visit is treated as though it were a vacation.

If you only see your partner regularly, you may feel compelled to make every minute of your time together count.

"You could feel tempted to treat it like vacation time," Cheatham adds, "especially if it's the only time you can have sex." While this is understandable, it makes it more difficult to know what your spouse is up to while you aren't around.

Don't overlook the minor details.

Make an effort to integrate daily events in your time together when you see each other in person:

- waking up to prepare breakfast
- assisting one another with chores
- falling asleep on the couch while watching a movie

Rather than hurrying from activity to activity, this peaceful intimacy might help you feel more connected.

Keeping your emotions and feelings to yourself

If you like to talk about challenging emotions or sentiments with your spouse in person, you may find it challenging to do so with a long-distance relationship. However, avoiding meaningful discussions can lead to problems in the long run.

Scott Cubberly, MSW, LCSW, adds, "Your ability and willingness to communicate about tough situations or feelings are both very crucial." "Many people avoid these situations because they are frightened of causing emotion or upheaval."

Furthermore, the lack of facial expressions or body language might make it easy to misinterpret statements or intentions, increasing the likelihood of misunderstandings.

Despite these challenges, it's critical to develop the habit of openly discussing your feelings with your partner. It won't benefit either of you in the long term if you avoid it or lie about how you feel.

IDENTIFYING AND RESOLVING COMMON PROBLEMS

Every relationship possesses its ups and downs, but physical distance can provide some unique challenges.

Here are some of the most common issues you could have, along with some recommendations to help you deal with them.

Relationship expectations vary.

Even the firmest relationship goals can alter over time; it never hurts to talk about what you intend to get out of the relationship at the start.

Shannon Batts, LMFT, adds, "Your expectations should correspond." "Are you doing this just for the joy of it, with no intention of making a long-term commitment?" Do you just want a fling or a close friend? Or do you want to improve your relationship abilities and create a shared life, even marriage? Have these discussions as soon as possible."

She also recommends that you keep the conversation going to ensure that you are both on the same page about where you want your relationship to go. If things don't feel quite right, don't be hesitant to reassess your initial expectations.

Issues of trust

It's possible that you (or your companion) won't be able to respond to texts or phone calls right away. However, you may discover that when you do speak with them, they appear distracted or uninterested. If this becomes a habit, you may grow concerned, even envious, if you know they spend a lot of time with other people.

These emotions are common, but they must be addressed. Cubberly emphasizes the importance of trust. "Openness and honesty, as well as responsiveness, can assist in developing trust. The mind fills in the holes with negatives if you aren't responsive."

When you bring up these worries, he recommends paying attention to your partner's reactions. "Do they appear open and unafraid? Do they understand your concerns?"

A partner is more invested in the relationship than the other.

It's hard for one person to maintain a relationship on their own. Even if one of you has greater responsibilities, both of you are responsible for the relationship's upkeep.

If you're the one who schedules all of the visits, initiates communication, and sends surprise care packages, you'll quickly become frustrated. You may also feel insecure in your relationship as a result of it.

Is there a solution to this problem? On both sides, better communication is needed. Discuss whether one of you has less emotional energy as a result of work duties or stress. Possessing an open and honest discussion about what you can both actually offer will alleviate some of the stress and ensure that you both feel safe.

Conflict avoidance

Conflict is something that most people dislike, especially in relationships. If you don't see or talk to your spouse as much as you'd want, you'll be even more hesitant to argue and will do everything you can to keep calls and visits nice.

Long-distance partnerships are more likely to have less conflict. Disagreements about errands or home chores, for example, are unlikely to arise. However, if you disagree with someone, expressing yourself is necessary, especially regarding personal values or serious issues.

Strongly conflicting points of view can cause friction, but they can also help you identify when a relationship isn't going to work out in the long run. So even if you think you might disagree with each other, don't be afraid to have difficult conversations.

Trying to maintain your relationship flawless and free of conflict can mask incompatibility or prevent you from progressing as partners.

Feeling disconnected from each other's life

Even if you and your partner are deeply engaged, the physical distance between you and your partner might make it appear like you live separate lives.

Cheatham argues that "creating a sense of shared life" is a distinct difficulty that can arise. "It is too easy to assume that you know everything about your partner's life, including their employment, their friends, and their daily routines. In a long-distance relationship, this can be difficult.

To close the distance, keep each other updated on your everyday activities. For example, tell stories about your coworkers or what happened on your commute. Discuss your friends' activities, your most recent hike, or what you're having for dinner. Sharing images of friends, pets, or items about the house can also assist in bridging the emotional gap.

"Even though you're in different cities," he continues, "there should be some sense that you're in each other's thoughts and hearts."

Expectations regarding money

If you want to see each other regularly, you may need to devote a lot of time and money. Even if you take turns booking time off work and paying for a vacation, those costs can rapidly pile up.

Cheatham advises those thinking about a long-distance relationship to consider these practical considerations. "These problems do not have to be deal-breakers," he says, "but they might develop animosity if they come as a surprise."

Financial issues aren't always easy to talk about, but it's a good idea to establish your expectations for visits early on in the relationship. Instead of attempting to stretch your budget, explain upfront that you can't afford to see your partner more than once a month.

A relationship does not have to end because of distance. Sure, you'll have to put in a little extra work and get creative with how you remain in touch, but you might discover that those features only serve to strengthen your bond.

THE MATTER OF CHOICE IN LONG DISTANCE RELATIONSHIPS

Have you ever met someone who insisted that no matter how hard you tried, a long-distance relationship would never work? It sounds even more familiar when they conclude the conversation with a catchphrase like "I know it because I've seen a lot of failed LDR." If you choose to listen to such comments, you will fail in your long-distance relationship because you will never be able to make it work. The reason is simple: you choose to obey the incorrect command or believe the incorrect concept.

I truly believe that everyone in the world has a perspective that is always the best for them. Because they are capable of only thinking the truth, what they think is true to them. I don't blame them because, at least in their own little world, they are correct. It's totally up to us whether we believe what is said or that every outcome is in our control. Let me tell you something: in a long-distance relationship, you have complete control over the outcome. The way you think about what you do can have a big impact on the outcome of your LDR. Your LDR journey will become easier or more predictable if you choose to believe that you can control the outcome of your long-distance relationship.

Here are some examples of positive decisions you can make in your long-distance relationship.

1) *Have faith in yourself, your partner, and the relationship as a whole.*

Nothing beats the trust and faith you had in yourself, your partner, and the relationship throughout a long-distance relationship. You could make all the preparations you want, but if you don't believe your long-distance relationship will work, nothing else matters. As a result, despite all the odds stacked against your relationship, you must choose to think that it will succeed.

2) *Taking a step back can help you strengthen your relationship.*

There's no such thing as a perfect romantic relationship, and long-distance partnerships are no exception. Setbacks are unavoidable in any relationship, but how you tune yourself to view them is crucial. You have the option of viewing it negatively or favorably, and the outcome (solutions) of your decision will influence the course of your relationship. As a result, rather than seeing the setback as a burden or a threat to your long-distance relationship, you should see it as an opportunity to strengthen it.

3) *You have the option of winning or losing.*

Due to a lack of self-confidence and uncertainty, we are inclined to notice only the negative aspects. We do not blame you for thinking this way; most long-distance couples we work with have expressed similar concerns. However, did you know that couples in long-distance relationships have the same success rate as couples in other types of relationships? According to studies, long-distance relationships have a success rate of up to 85 percent. With this information, you can choose to be in the 85 percent positive group or the 15 percent failure group. If you're passionate about your long-distance relationship, you should count yourself among the 85 percent who succeed.

4) *Long-distance opportunity*

In a long-distance relationship, physical distance is not always detrimental to the relationship. Physical distance stops you from engaging in certain physical behaviors like hand-holding, kissing, embracing, and intercourse, but it does not hinder you from moving further in the relationship. Physical separation is an excellent opportunity for you to find your relationship and yourself. While your partner is away, you can always use the time to improve yourself by enrolling in classes you've always wanted to take, and so on.

In fact, the distance will put your patience, as well as your love for your partner and the relationship's integrity, to the test. As a result, instead of placing focus on what you can't accomplish because of the distance, you may always focus on how you can strengthen your connection from afar. What you choose here could have a big impact on whether or not you're happy in your long-distance relationship.

5) *Communication issues.*

This is one of the vital factors that can make or destroy a long-distance relationship. Unfortunately, many people assume they will not succeed in communication because of the obstacles, effort, and money involved. Instead of focusing on the difficulties, consider the opportunities that present themselves. The most important thing to learn here is how to communicate effectively over long distances. Distance will instantly increase your communication skills; therefore, you won't be able to learn this vital talent anywhere else. All other issues described earlier can be readily overcome with current technology if you start thinking properly (Internet, VOIP phone, email, etc.). As a result, you've got the freedom to choose what is best for you in terms of long-distance communication once again.

There are two sides to all coins, and the options listed above are only a few of the options presented to you in your long-distance relationship. Throughout a long-distance relationship, how or what you choose has a significant effect.

You have a choice, and if you make the right one, you will succeed in any relationship.

LONG DISTANCE RELATIONSHIPS - FAQS

I believe you will agree with me when I say that long-distance relationships may be quite difficult.

Is that the case? Well, it turns out that knowing a few simple facts will drastically boost your chances of having a happy, healthy, and rewarding long-distance relationship. For example, how often should you see one another, what I advise AGAINST doing, and do long-distance relationships work at all?

Long-distance relationships: how prevalent are they?

Statistics on Long-Distance Relationships: In 2005 (the most recent statistics available), the best estimates imply that

3,569,000 married people in the United States lived apart for reasons other than marital strife (the latest data available). This represents 2.9 percent of all marriages in the United States.

There were 839,000 more people in long-distance marriages in 2005 than there were in 2000. Between 2000 and 2005, there was a 30% increase in the number of long-distance marriages (2.36 percent of marriages in 2000 and 2.9 percent of marriages in 2005). (2.36 percent of marriages in 2000 against 2.9 percent in 2005).

Newlyweds had a higher risk of being long-distance early in their marriage, with one research of 600 couples finding that one in ten were long-distance for at least part of their first three years.

Pre-marital couples are more challenging to research, even though an estimated 4.4 million college students are in LDRs (20-40% of all students in various studies). According to one survey, one in every seven (14%) romantic relationships is long-distance. According to census data, 3.5 million dating couples are likely to be long-distance. Thus, approximately 7 million couples (14-15 million people) in the United States feel they are in a long-distance relationship.

Is it becoming increasingly common to have long-distance relationships?

In 2005, there were 839,000 more long-distance marriages than there were in 2000. Between 2000 and 2005, there was a

23% increase in long-distance marriages (2.36 percent of marriages in 2000 and 2.9 percent of marriages in 2005). Part of this development can be attributed to increased exposure to singles from other countries.

"People travel for work, they commute longer distances, and they travel more in general than we did only a few decades ago. All of these factors heighten the likelihood that they may fall for someone who does not live nearby, according to Dr. Guldner.

The proliferation of Internet dating services has inevitably resulted in forming "coast-to-coast couples" – people who reside on various sides of the country who met online but have a real, not just virtual, relationship. Thus, long-distance relationships are finally being accepted as a realistic option by society.

As a result, not only are there more long-distance sparks flying these days, but people are also considerably more willing to light the flames of these romances rather than dismiss them.

Do LDRs work? Is it possible to have a long-distance relationship?

LDRs do not break up at a higher rate than more typical, geographically near couples, contrary to popular belief.

Several researchers comparing LDRs to geographically close couples have discovered that the breakup rates are the same over time.

Break-up Rates for Long-Distance Relationships (LDRs) vs. Proximal (Close) Relationships (PR) from 5 Studies

- Over the course of six months, 30 percent PR and 27 percent LDR were achieved.
- Over the course of three months, 21% PR vs. 37% LDR*
- Over 6 months, 35 percent PR vs. 42 percent LDR*
- Over 6 months, PR was 23% vs. LDR was 11%.
- Over the course of a year, 25% PR vs. 8% LDR

*There is no statistically significant difference between the rates (i.e., they are statistically equal)

Is it true that couples in LDRs have less fulfilling relationships?

Several studies have compared couples in LDRs to couples in geographically close relationships in order to assess relationship quality.

Couples in Long Distance Relationships report the same levels of pleasure, intimacy, trust, and commitment in their relationships.

How frequently should long-distance spouses see one other?

This is just one of several inquiries concerning the demography of long-distance relationships, such as how far away couples live, how often they visit or call one another, how long they were together as a geographically close couple before having to separate, and so on.

I divide long-distance relationships into four categories: demography, the personality of each pair member, the relationship's support structure, and the relationship's overall quality.

According to research, demographics have the most negligible impact on the success or failure of a long-distance relationship of these four factors.

Couples therapists who specialize in long-distance relationships have naturally recommended frequent face-to-face meetings. However, when researchers looked into this further, the largest and best-designed studies revealed no link between the frequency with which couples visit one another and their likelihood of staying together. I recognize that this defies logic, therefore in the book (Long Distance Relationships), I go over each of the studies that looked into this issue in greater depth. Unfortunately, this is only one of countless findings from studies that contradict the views of many "experts."

The great news is that couples should feel free to visit each other as frequently as they can afford.

Because of our hectic work schedules, my LDR partner and I don't get to speak often. As a result, we don't get to chat much on some days, which can be quite challenging.

We well understand the pressures that come with juggling a busy job schedule and also maintaining an LDR. Our recommendation is to schedule times to chat with each other, such as reserving time in each of your calendars for a date. This may be challenging, but setting out time to communicate together gives you something to look forward to and may force you to stay in touch. If you don't have time to talk, attempt to keep the conversation going using SMS or emails. This will allow you to speak with each other whenever you have the opportunity.

My long-distance partner and I have yet to meet in person. I'm starting to feel like I'm losing interest in continuing the connection. Should I press my spouse for a face-to-face meeting?

Although you can start a good relationship without meeting someone in person, it is necessary to meet face to face eventually. A bond formed only online may not necessarily be maintained in the real world.

We frequently hear about long-distance couples who discover that their connection isn't as strong as they had thought after meeting for the first time. You don't want to put a lot of time or effort into a relationship that you're not sure about. If you feel you need to meet your long-distance relationship in person to be sure it is something you wish to pursue, you should definitely let your long-distance partner know.

If you have affections for your spouse, they should want to meet you as much as you want to meet them. I wouldn't suggest pressuring or forcing your spouse to meet you;

instead, let them know why you believe it's necessary and agree on a time that works for both of you.

When you haven't met your partner in person, it might be difficult to sustain your passion for a long-distance relationship, so don't be scared to try to keep it alive by meeting together. A meeting could provide you with the information you need to decide whether to stay in the relationship or move on.

What are the tips on how to deal with concerns and the unknown in a long-distance relationship?

The most important piece of advice we can offer is to avoid overthinking or forcing anything. You want your long-distance romance to grow organically, just like a regular relationship would. Long-distance relationships can be challenging, so don't expect to have all the answers right once.

Relationships are exciting in part because you never know where they may lead. Life is long; don't feel obligated to figure it all out at an early age. If your long-distance relationship does end, simply take what you've learned and move on. When the moment is right, you'll find the one who is a better match for you.

Too many people strive to control the unknown, which only keeps them from living in the present. Accept that there'll be many unknowns, and have a cheerful attitude to help you get through them. Your relationship is likely to fail if you are gloomy. So always try to keep a happy attitude while also having realistic expectations.

I want to meet my long-distance boyfriend, but I have never traveled far from home before. I am terrified to fly, and a really long journey separates us. How can I conquer this fear?

Long-distance relationships can demand you to move way outside of your comfort zone. At some moment you will have to meet each other if there will be a future for you both. If your partner is able and ready to go to you first, this is definitely your best option in order to be sure the relationship is actually something you want to pursue.

You might also explore your partner traveling to you, where they could see how you live, and then both of you could fly together to see where and how they live. But, again, having your lover near you may assist in lessening the fear of flying and keep your thoughts engaged.

Alternatively, you might ask a close family member or friend to travel with you to meet your partner. This provides you assistance while traveling and during your visit. If the meeting between you and your spouse goes wrong, you will still have someone present for you who could be brilliant in terms of safety. Even if your long-distance romance doesn't play out in the real world, you and your traveling companion could still enjoy a holiday together.

My older kids are very much against my long-distance relationship since they feel that it was the reason for my divorcing their father. What should I do?

Without knowing the circumstances regarding how your marriage to their father ended in divorce, it is fairly tough to understand why they may feel this way. However, whatever the reason for your separation from your children's father, you definitely took the decision because you were unhappy with your shared relationship.

Moving forward, your top goal should be focusing on your new long-distance relationship and ensuring your own satisfaction. If your children have grown up and become self-sufficient, they should concentrate on their own life. Of course, you should be sensitive to their feelings and willing to answer any questions they may have. If you give to them time and space, they may come to terms with your new relationship.

The most important thing, I believe, is to not force your new relationship on your children. Allow them to determine when they're ready to meet your new spouse and attempt to understand why they're upset from their perspective. Above all, avoid interfering with their bond with their father. Finally, try to be respectful of your ex-husband and don't compel them to take sides.

My long-distance girlfriend accuses me of being juvenile in my love gestures. I've written him old-fashioned love letters and sent him modest, thoughtful presents, but he doesn't seem to like or appreciate anything I've sent him. Is there something I'm missing?

Everyone will have a unique personality, but you must remain true to yourself. You shouldn't feel compelled to hide your feelings for your partner or the methods you want to show it.

You should have a conversation with your partner to figure out why he doesn't enjoy your gestures. Maybe he's humiliated because you're putting in more effort than he can or understands. On the other hand, it's common for males to want to sweep women off their feet, so it could simply be a matter of him feeling emasculated.

If he simply does not appreciate or like your thoughtfulness, you should consider whether he is the ideal person for you.

My long-distance partner and I are engaged, although we have yet to meet. We love and trust one other, but my pals are perplexed about how I can truly know him without meeting him.

Before you jump into anything, we propose that you get to know him better. You may feel as if you know someone before meeting them in person, but you must spend time with them in person to determine if you are compatible. In-person, people's personalities may be radically different from the one they project online. It's impossible to predict how you'll conduct as a couple without first spending time with one other.

This isn't to imply that your relationship won't work out; nevertheless, you might want to take things a little slower at first. Before rushing into an engagement, it would have been prudent for you both to meet. Before committing to a person for the rest of your life, you must be 100 percent certain. It appears that being 100 percent certain about someone you haven't met in person would be a challenging endeavor.

My LDR spouse appears to be less confident in the success of our long-distance relationship than I am. So how do I give her hope that we'll be able to work things out?

Make it clear to her that you are entirely committed to making the relationship work. Try not to overburden her with discussions about your future together, as this will likely cause her concern. The more we try to think about things like marriage, relocating, changing jobs, selling houses, and having children, the more we may fear the situation is too much for us to handle or figure out.

Take every day as it comes and try to enjoy yourself with your partner. Of course, the details of your future will fall into place over time, but for now, the most important thing is to focus on getting to know each other and making your time together joyful.

Be willing to address any questions she may have along the road and give her time to think things over independently. You won't force her into anything she doesn't want to do if you truly love her. On the other hand, if she decides that the relationship is too much for her to bear at this time, don't write it off totally.

Allow your spouse some space to consider whether the relationship is something she wants to fight for or whether she wants to end it. If you both decide to leave the relationship or take a break, don't be scared to move on as well. Instead of waiting for your partner to alter her mind, look into other possibilities that might be better suited to your needs.

The parents of my LDR spouse are vehemently opposed to our long-distance relationship. We have been together for a long time and are planning to marry one day. I don't want to be the one who causes my partner's family to perish. So, what should I do now?

Whether or not your boyfriend chooses to stay with you or listens to his parents' counsel is a choice he must make. You should talk with him in which you express that you appreciate how difficult the decision is and that you don't want to be the cause of a family feud.

If he chooses you above his family, you should never feel bad as long as you did not put any pressure on him to make the decision. Instead, you need to have an open and honest chat with him, explaining that you don't want to end up in a condition where he blames you for your choices.

In the best-case scenario, your partner's parents will eventually come to terms with you and your relationship. Unfortunately, parents are frequently too protective of their children and merely want to ensure that they have a nice life. Continue to treat your partner's parents with respect and courtesy, so they have no reason to detest you.

Your partner is the only person who truly needs to be concerned about you. You'll be alright as long as he believes in your partnership and is willing to battle for what you both have.

My long-distance relationship has been criticized by many of my friends and family members. What can I do to help them understand and support their decision?

The most vital piece of advice we could provide you for dealing with negativity from family and friends is to make a vow to yourself that you will not be affected. Allowing bad energy to undermine your relationship is not a good idea. It will be challenging at first, but with practice, it will become easier. Your friends and family will grow accustomed to the notion as your relationship matures, and the unfavorable comments should begin to fade.

Your partner is likely struggling with the same negativity. Have a dialogue about it so that you can encourage one another. Seek out friends or family members who will support you and will not pass judgment on your actions.

When people don't understand a problem, they tend to be negative. They may also be opposed to your relationship because they care about you and believe they advocate for your best interests. Make it obvious that you appreciate their concern but know this is the right relationship for you.

Although it would be wonderful to acquire their support in the long run, you don't require it for your relationship to thrive. You could be confident that your relationship will work out if both you and your partner believe in it. You should never feel obligated to justify your relationship. Simply live your life and allow your friends and family to accept you as you are.

Of course, you should always be receptive to your family's opinions and worries in case they notice something that you don't. Respect what they have to say, but remember that it is ultimately up to you to decide what you wish to do with your life.

Is it true that couples in long-distance relationships are more likely to cheat on each other?

One of the most common concerns among long-distance couples is that their partner (or they) may have an affair while they are apart.

According to common sense, couples who can't keep an eye on each other are more likely to wander. Therefore, researchers looked into whether long-distance couples had more affairs than couples that live close together. Unfortunately, this research yielded both positive and negative results. The good news is that all three studies found that long-distance couples had no higher risk of having an affair than couples who lived near together. Thus, it appears that the likelihood of having an affair is determined more by the quality of the couple's relationship and the personalities involved than by chance.

The sad news is that, contrary to popular belief, those in long-distance relationships are much more concerned about affairs than those in geographically close relationships.

Is there anything you would recommend avoiding?

Yes. Don't socially isolate yourself. Don't stress about how often you can or can't see each other; the study suggests that it doesn't make a difference.

Don't be concerned about infidelity; people cheat because of personality conflicts or relationship problems, not because of distance. Take other people's counsel with a grain of salt – there are no "musts" in long-distance relationships. LDRs are more similar than dissimilar to typical relationships. Don't allow someone to convince you that you "must" talk to each other every night or visit each other once a month. This is not the case, according to the study.

Many people emphasize the need to maintain separate lives rather than simply waiting for the partner to get home.

Yes. Separate lives help long-distance relationships in a variety of ways. It contributes to socialization, which we've already discussed. One of the many benefits of an LDR is that it helps you be productive and grow. According to our research, compared to those in geographically near relationships, people in LDRs who were in school were generally more successful. They felt their education to be more fascinating, enjoyable, and constructive. Couples can still have an intimate loving relationship with the one they love while also developing in ways they wouldn't otherwise be able to. Researchers have used the term "compartmentalization" to describe how couples in LDRs communicate about it. This refers to psychologically separating their lives into two compartments: one for when they're together with their spouse and the other for when they're separated. When separated, they enter the "apart" compartment and concentrate on work, self-improvement, or socializing; thoughts about the spouse are there but not dominant. This aids them in coping with the separation on a psychological level. Those who simply "sit by the phone" haven't formed an "apart" compartment, and they continue to live in the "together" world even when they aren't.

This consumes a significant amount of psychological energy that may be put to better use.

Is there a link between distance and some issues, such as envy, misunderstandings, and so on?

Yes, distance can exacerbate some problems.

Even though we know that couples in LDRs do not cheat on one another any more than couples in close proximity geographically, we also know that LDRs are more concerned about cheating.

They sometimes build a fantasy world in which their partner is cheating since they are unable to visually watch their spouse in the same way that a geographically near couple can. This fantasy is frequently shattered in a geographically near relationship when couples unconsciously or deliberately monitor one another. In an LDR, monitoring is far more difficult, and imaginations can quickly spiral out of control.

Furthermore, as I previously stated, telephone usage can lead to more misconceptions due to the lack of visual clues. Facial expressions, hand movements, and body position all transmit a great deal of information. All of this is lost over the phone, and even a simple comment can be misinterpreted. Also, as previously said, some LDR couples are hesitant to discuss certain things for fear of "rocking the boat" or "sabotaging" their time together.

As a result, when a topic is misinterpreted, they may fail to confront the issue, leading to it escalating into something far more serious than before.

What is the most difficult aspect of long-distance relationships?

Maintaining the feeling of simply being a part of each other's lives is the most challenging aspect of a long-distance relationship.

Couples who only get to see each other once a week or once a month may feel estranged from their partner. Intimacy can be eroded as a result of this separation. Consider intimacy to have two components:

1) emotional exchange and

2) interconnectedness of daily activities. Couples in long-distance relationships (LDRs) are usually excellent at sharing their feelings for each other. However, the second part of the equation, "interconnectedness," necessitates a significant amount of effort. Interconnectedness entails being involved in your partner's day-to-day activities, adventures, problems, and accomplishments, which are frequently banal.

Couples who live near one other do this nearly subconsciously when they talk about prospective or current occurrences.

When these small occurrences are addressed at the moment, they seem interesting and exciting, but they lose their interest and excitement when they are addressed afterward. "Guess what occurred to me in the grocery store?" for example, would be a comment shared later that night between geographically near couples. The unconscious connection built between couples with each small encounter, such as this, provides the foundation of intimacy, despite the content's triviality. However, in a long-distance relationship, the same couple would either forget about this little event at the grocery store or discover it has lost its appeal when brought up several days later.

Intimacy reminds me of a rope that binds two individuals together. The exchanging of feelings with one another is the rope's fundamental core. However, thousands of small threads are made up of each seemingly insignificant exchange or experience between a pair surrounding this core. While no single fiber is particularly vital, they form the fundamental strength of the relationship when taken together. Couples in LDRs usually have a strong inner core, but it isn't enough to keep the couple together on its own.

They must put in a lot of effort to add the outer strands by learning to partake in each other's world even when separated.

POSITIVE HABITS TO IMPROVE YOUR LDR

Keep a positive attitude!

When we looked at dozens of coping techniques employed by long-distance couples, the one that stood out was maintaining a positive attitude toward the relationship. When I deal with long-distance couples, I stress the importance of debunking falsehoods, challenging naysayers, and focusing on the positive. Research reveals that LDRs have no higher risk of breaking up than any other type of relationship despite popular belief. Traditional couples report exactly as much satisfaction, intimacy, trust, and commitment as LDRs.

Sexual affairs are not more common in LDRs than in other relationships. LDRs are not a "poor idea"; in fact, they are frequently the greatest option among those available. Couples must not merely put up with others who tell them LDRs "never work" to challenge the naysayers. Inquire as to how they know this, as research indicates that this is not the case. We wouldn't tolerate someone saying our geographically near relationship was "doomed," so don't say the same thing about our LDR.

Focusing on the positive encourages couples to consider the many benefits that come with an LDR.

Re-Learn What It Means to Be Intimate

This relates to your first question's response. In order to bond, couples in LDRs frequently spend their precious time together or on the phone to convey sincere emotions. However, they don't pay attention to the small details that make us feel connected and close. According to our findings, what couples say and the way they say it matters considerably more than how often they talk.

To re-learn intimacy, we take a five-step strategy.

• First, find methods to participate in the small, everyday activities. If the couple has access to email, send one in the morning to discuss the day's plans and another in the evening to report on how things went. Couples that communicate every night should discuss how their day went and their plans for the next day. Couples who have limited contact can keep a journal of issues they'd like to discuss with their partner the next time they speak. Without it, these insignificant experiences will fade from memory.

Keep note of your partner's activities as well, so you may inquire about them and feel included. For example, some couples "talk" with their partners throughout the day using hand-held tape recorders. The recording is then sent to the partner, who can now feel connected to the world of their spouse. Although many couples express significant emotions on these records, the actual focus should be on day-to-day conversation. Some couples use Polaroid photos or digital camera photos to show their partner the tiny things that happen during the day.

• Second, technology may be used to promote intimacy. Couples in geographically close relationships naturally establish intimacy by chatting with one another while doing other things. This generates a sense of "being in the world together," distinct from the sentiments experienced when two people are completely focused on each other. Purchase a hands-free cordless phone (costs between $50 and $99 in the United States). This allows you to do laundry, tidy up, or do other duties while conversing with your partner (in the academic field, this is referred to as "parallel communication"). This can drastically alter the tone of a phone call and result in far deeper intimacy in the long run. According to our research, couples in LDRs who stayed together wrote to each other twice as often as those who broke up (even when we controlled for differences in trust, commitment, etc.) Handwritten letters (rather than emails) have a psychological effect that promotes intimacy. For some couples, scenting these letters with a certain cologne or perfume can have a significant impact.

• Be aware of the dangers of conversing on the phone. Unfortunately, studies reveal that conversing on the phone has some significant disadvantages. Arguments are more difficult to resolve, viewpoints are harder to foresee, couples feel misunderstood and attacked, and they may regard their partner as less sincere and intelligent than when they speak face to face. Couples must learn to recognize tiny issues that arise while on the phone and distinguish between issues that arise from merely utilizing the phone and those that are more significant.

• Remind yourself of your lover on a regular basis. When your lover can't be physically present, there are various ways to keep them psychologically close. The most obvious are images, but you can also purchase talking photos in which your companion leaves a digitally recorded message that could be replayed at the touch of a button. Digital key chains are cheap and can record several seconds of your partner's voice. Digital video telephones, which deliver a live picture of your companion every few seconds while you converse on the phone, are more expensive. Cards or letters with a favorite aroma can assist by engaging a third sense in addition to sight and sound.

Some things must be said.

LDR couples frequently avoid discussing subjects that are crucial to their relationships. Couples frequently don't want to "sacrifice" a weekend by bringing up difficulties because they only have so much time together. As a result, there's a tendency to put off discussing serious issues (frequently indefinitely).

According to research, while LDR couples dispute less frequently than normal couples, they also progress more slowly. Couples in LDRs might also come to idealize their relationship (while downplaying the bad aspects), which works fine until they reunite. Disillusionment can then set in. To counteract this, we propose that couples set aside time to talk about their relationship and resolve any issues that may arise. One frequently overlooked item is "ground rules" for engaging with others that could be seen as a danger to the relationship. Is it, for example, acceptable to go out to dinner with someone? Is it acceptable to see a movie together? Some dating couples even permit their partners to date other people. Our research discovered that about 30% of couples who discussed ground rules ended up breaking up, regardless of whether they went on to date other people or not. However, 70% of couples that did not discuss this issue ended up divorcing. Finally, we advise couples in LDRs to acknowledge their partners' contributions freely.

LDR men, in particular, believe that their partners have failed to recognize their achievements.

Refrain from isolating yourself!

According to studies, people who live in LDRs typically isolate themselves from others. Work serves as a diversion from their loneliness. When they're out in public, they feel self-conscious. Their ambiguous status – physically unattached but not romantically available – might be unsettling in some social contexts. When people are out in public and watch other couples having fun, they can feel lonely. Those in LDRs frequently have to focus on work while separated in order to have time to spend with their partner when they are together. When people are separated, all of these factors lead to a predisposition to withdraw. We do know, though, that the amount of social support received from friends and family affects both the emotional difficulty experienced while separated and the chances of the partnership being intact. As a result, we encourage persons living in LDRs to make an effort to socialize and spend time with friends. We've also discovered that having a confidant is crucial.

A confidant is a buddy (not a love partner) with whom you may securely discuss relationship difficulties and other relevant matters.

Be Prepared for Disappointment.

Couples in long-distance relationships (LDRs) may judge the success of their relationship based on the perceived quality of their most recent time together. If the weekend goes well, the relationship is in good shape, and if the weekend was a letdown, the relationship is in jeopardy.

Every relationship possesses its ups and downs, and geographically near relationships can absorb these ups and downs more easily by simply spending more time together. In between "down" times, separated spouses may languish in despair or anxiety.

Knowing that there will be some frustrating times together – and that this is to be expected – will help you get through those less-than-ideal weekends.

Lastly, master the art of long-distance sex.

Couples therapists understand that a couple's sexual experience typically mirrors and predicts the overall intimacy of their relationship. Fortunately, research has shown that couples living in LDRs have just as good sex lives as couples living close. Couples in LDRs frequently experience a "honeymoon" effect on reconnecting, complete with passionate and novel sexual escapades (one of the advantages of LDRs). Couples who are separated must learn to be sexual without being physically close. This usually takes the form of phone sex, sexy letters, photographs, or movies. When working with couples in long-distance relationships, I frequently examine each person's comfort level with the concept of long-distance sex. Do they think it's okay to talk "erotically" on the phone? Are they at ease with self-gratification? We work on making them cooler with long-distance sex if they want to make it a part of their relationship. They can begin by listening to sexual fantasies over the phone (or even just to themselves first).

People can even learn how to write erotic fantasies from literature. The sexual component of a relationship can sometimes be so crucial to one or both partners that the quality of telephone sex can make or break it.

CONCLUSION

Being in a long-distance relationship is complicated. Many people are unable to cope with the stress or the distance. However, some people are fortunate enough to have nice, loving, and patient spouses willing to spend time with me. If you find yourself in a long-distance relationship, keep these three crucial elements in mind. Communication, honesty, and patience are all important. When two individuals truly love each other, the miles between them are only a minor nuisance because you know what you have is worth more than the miles.

Finally, I'd want to wish you all the best in your long-distance relationship!

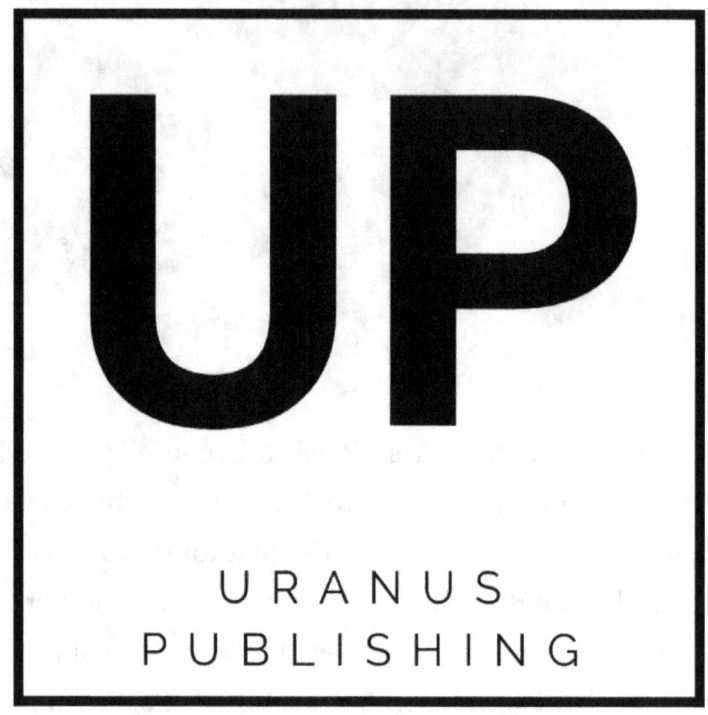